# DONALD DEWAR

## *A Book of Tribute*

PUBLISHED IN A LIMITED EDITION OF 1500 COPIES.

THIS COPY IS NUMBER

1255

OF

Applications for reproduction should be made in writing to The Stationery Office Limited
St Crispins, Duke Street, Norwich NR3 1PD.

The information contained in the publication is believed to be correct at time of manufacture. Whilst care has been taken to
ensure that the information is accurate, the publisher can accept no responsibility for any errors or omissions or for change to
the details given.

A CIP catalogue record for this book is available from the British Library.
A Library of congress CIP catalogue record has been applied for.

First Published 2000

ISBN 033 880024 7

Photographs on page 3 and 15 © Press Associatiom

The Scottish
Parliament

# FOREWORD

To all who knew and loved him, Donald Dewar was a great man.

Sadly missed by his colleagues in The Scottish Parliament, he was regarded as a fine leader, an extraordinary politician and a formidable debater.

His heartfelt speeches and his witty ripostes often gave life to the parliamentary chamber.

This book tries, in a small way, to capture how his friends, colleagues and others regarded him.

It also includes a selection of his inspirational speeches, which I know will serve as a reminder to all who read them of the genuine and passionate man that was Donald Dewar.

**David Steel**
Presiding Officer

*"A leader of a party, country and parliament whose legacy will be for all time"*

(Source: Scottish Parliament Condolence Book)

# DONALD DEWAR
## *1937 - 2000*

*As a close friend and colleague, Murray Elder knew Donald Dewar better than most. This biography of the late First Minister also acts as his tribute to the man who brought Devolution to Scotland.*

Donald Campbell Dewar was born in Glasgow in 1937. His parents were elderly, and had little choice but to send him to a boarding school in the Borders when ill-health affected them both.

After a few years he returned to Glasgow, to finish his education at Glasgow Academy. He went late to Glasgow University - he often said that his headmaster told his parents that he 'would benefit from a university education if he were lucky enough to gain an entry qualification'.

He studied history and then law, playing an active role in the University Labour Club and the now-famous University Union and its Debating Society. It was there that he first met fellow students, including John Smith, many of whom were destined for careers in public life, and who would become his life-long friends.

Donald was destined for a career in politics. His chance came in the 1966 General Election when he won a famous political victory in Aberdeen South - the first time Labour had ever won the traditionally Tory seat.

He lost the seat, narrowly, in 1970 and returned to Glasgow, to resume a career in the law as a reporter to the new children's panel system.

He had to wait another eight years before he could return to Westminster but did so following a second famous political victory in the by-election for Glasgow Garscadden in 1978. His victory was all the more significant given that it came at a time when Labour's national fortunes were at a low ebb and the Scottish National Party had made significant inroads in Scotland and in the seat. Donald's victory was a turning point for Labour in Scotland and just reward for the determined campaign he fought in the election. He never looked back.

From 1979 to 1981 he served as Chairman of the Scottish Affairs Select Committee. He was an Opposition Spokesman on Scottish Affairs for the next eleven years, becoming Shadow Secretary of State for Scotland from 1983 until 1992.

Over these years he was able to put his own stamp on the development of devolution policy, to which he had an unswerving committment.

In 1988 he took the brave and decisive step of taking Labour into the Scottish Constitutional Convention, committing himself to work with all other parties - not all of course, were prepared to accept the challenge of seeking to build a consensus across Scotland for a devolved parliament. The working relationship with the Liberal Party that emerged however was to bear fruit later in the formation of the partnership government in the first devolved administration after the Scottish elections in 1999.

His friend and colleague John Smith appointed him Labour spokesman on Social Security, and following his death, Tony Blair recognised the respect in which he was held by his fellow MPs, when he made him Labour Chief Whip (1995-97).

He became Secretary of State for Scotland after the 1997 election with the chance to deliver on Labour's promise of a Scottish Parliament. It was, he was happy to admit, a dream come true.

His influence over the shape and scope of the legislation to set up the Parliament was decisive - aided by what became to the suspicion of some, a close working relationship with Derry Irvine, the chair of the committee responsible for the legislation and because of their considerable efforts it was successfully steered through the Westminster Parliament.

A decisive referendum victory in Scotland followed.

Donald stood for election to the new Parliament which he had done so much to create, and was elected MSP for Glasgow Anniesland; and as the Party's Leader in Scotland, became the first First Minister. It was the high point of his career.

A man who was often uncomfortable with public displays of affection, was visibly touched by the public response on the opening day of the new Parliament. It was the culmination of years of his personal endeavour, he enjoyed it to the full, and that enjoyment was obvious to everyone who saw him.

During his period as First Minister, he was always keen to remind his colleagues that The Scottish Parliament was not an end in itself, but a means to an end - to deliver social justice.

It was the core of his own beliefs. And he was never afraid to hide his own instinctive liberal views on social policy issues, even in the face of media hostility. He stood firm and his determination and sense of purpose for what he believed to be right won through.

He never forgot the people who had given him their support. Throughout his distinguished career, he remained a hugely committed constituency MP, dealing assiduously with the problems of the people he had been elected to serve.

Earlier this year he had a heart valve replacement operation from which he made a good recovery, but in October after returning to his desk as First Minister he died of a sudden and massive brain haemorrhage. He was 63 and left a daughter and a son. Donald was also a grandfather and his grand daughter was a source of much pride and joy.

He had an encyclopaedic knowledge of Scottish art, was tremendously well read, and for all that politics dominated his life, had as wide interests, and as varied a circle of friends, as any one I have known. Companionable and witty, he was intensely loyal to his friends, and frankly failed to understand a lack of loyalty in others.

His funeral in Glasgow was one of the largest ever witnessed in Scotland with well over a thousand people from all walks of life packed into the aisles and the nave of Glasgow Cathedral. Many more thousands lined the route of the cortege as Donald's body took its last journey through his native City of Glasgow and through his own Constituency.

That day the people of Glasgow demonstrated clearly that the affection in which he held his fellow Glaswegians, was more than reciprocated.

He will be missed by many and not just those of us who were lucky enough to know him well.

Donald's deserved place in Scottish political history is assured.

*"Thank you for your honesty, integrity and inspiration"*

(Source: Scottish Parliament Condolence Book)

# A Moment Anchored in Our History

*Donald Dewar's speech to the Opening Ceremony of
The Scottish Parliament - 1 July 1999*

"There shall be a Scottish Parliament - I like that" Donald Dewar's famous comment about the opening sentence of The Scotland Act underlined - as if that were needed - his enthusiasm and determination to deliver devolution.

On 1 July 1999, the vision became a reality when Her Majesty The Queen arrived in a sun-kissed Edinburgh to open the new legislature at it's temporary home on The Mound.

This speech by Donald Dewar, in reply to Her Majesty's address, has been widely acclaimed as one of his finest.

> *Your Majesty; on behalf of the people of Scotland, I thank you for the gift of this mace.*
>
> *It is a symbol of the great democratic traditions from which we draw our inspiration and our strength.*
>
> *At its head are inscribed the opening words of our founding statute:*
>
> *'There shall be a Scottish Parliament'*
>
> *Through long years, those words were first a hope, then a belief, then a promise. Now, they are a reality.*
>
> *This is a moment anchored in our history.*

*Today, we reach back through the long haul to win this Parliament, through the struggles of those who brought democracy to Scotland, to that other Parliament dissolved in controversy nearly three centuries ago.*

*Today, we look forward to the time when this moment will be seen as a turning point: the day when democracy was renewed in Scotland, when we revitalised our place in this our United Kingdom.*

*This is about more than our politics and our laws. This is about who we are, how we carry ourselves. There is a new voice in the land, the voice of a democratic Parliament. A voice to shape Scotland as surely as the echoes from our past:*

*the shout of the welder in the din of the great Clyde shipyards;*

*the speak of the Mearns, with its soul in the land;*

*the discourse of the enlightenment, when Edinburgh and Glasgow were a light held to the intellectual life of Europe;*

*the wild cry of the Great Pipes;*

*and back to the distant cries of the battles of Bruce and Wallace.*

*Walter Scott wrote that only a man with soul so dead could have no sense, no feel of his native land. For me, for any Scot, today is a proud moment: a new stage on a journey begun long ago and which has no end. This is a proud day for all of us.*

*A Scottish Parliament. Not an end: a means to greater ends. And those too are part of our mace. Woven into its symbolic thistles are these four words:*

*'Wisdom. Justice. Compassion. Integrity.'*

*Burns would have understood that. We have just heard - beautifully sung - one of his most enduring works (A Man's a Man for a' That). At that heart of the song is a very Scottish conviction: that honesty and simple dignity are priceless virtues, not imparted by rank or birth or privilege but part of the soul.*

*Burns believed that sense and worth ultimately prevail. He believed that was the core of politics; that without it, ours would be an impoverished profession.*

*'Wisdom. Justice. Compassion. Integrity.' Timeless values. Honourable aspirations for this new forum of democracy, born on the cusp of a new century.*

*We are fallible. We will make mistakes. But we will never lose sight of what brought us here: the striving to do right by the people of Scotland; to respect their priorities; to better their lot; and to contribute to the commonweal.*

*I look forward to the days ahead when this Chamber will sound with debate, argument and passion. When men and women from all over Scotland will meet to work together for a future built from the first principles of social justice.*

*But today, we pause and reflect. It is a rare privilege in an old nation to open a new Parliament. Today is a celebration of the principles, the traditions, the democratic imperatives which have brought us to this point and will sustain us into the future.*

*Your Majesty, we are all proud that you are here to handsel this Parliament and with us as we dedicate ourselves to the work ahead.*

*Your Majesty, our thanks.*

*"You set a very fine example of decency in politics"*

(Source: Scottish Parliament Condolence Book)

# TRIBUTES IN THE SCOTTISH PARLIAMENT
## *13 October 2000*

On the afternoon of Friday 13 October, MSPs gathered at the Assembly Hall in Edinburgh for a special meeting of Parliament, which heard tributes from the Presiding Officer and representatives of the four main political parties.

The following motion of condolence, moved by Acting First Minister Jim Wallace MSP, was approved:

> *"That the Parliament expresses its deep regret and sadness at the untimely death of its First Minister, The Rt Hon Donald Dewar MP, MSP; offers its sympathy and sincere condolences to his family and many friends whose grief is shared by all members of this Parliament; agrees that tributes should be paid to a distinguished Parliamentarian and great leader of Scotland; further agrees that as a mark of respect no other business will be taken today."*

After observing one minute's silence, the following tributes were made:

# The Rt.hon SIR DAVID STEEL MSP
*Presiding Officer of The Scottish Parliament*

This is not a meeting that any of us would have wished to hold. The news of our First Minister's death came with such devastating suddenness, after we had all assumed that he had come safely through his serious heart operation.

It is cruel how Scotland has been robbed in recent years of so many able politicians in their prime: John P Mackintosh (Labour); Alick Buchanan-Smith (Conservative); Allan Macartney (SNP); John Smith (Labour); and now Donald Dewar.

Donald, however, at least had the satisfaction of leaving behind the completion of what he described as first a hope, then a belief, then a promise and then a reality - the restoration of Scotland's Parliament after 300 years.

He questioned the title 'father of the nation', but he was without question the father of the Parliament. Under his leadership, this new Parliament had already found its head, its energy and its skills. Today, as it meets to mourn his death, it has found its heart.

Over the past two days, hundreds of tributes have been paid to Donald Dewar, so many that it is difficult to find anything new to say about him. We do not need to find anything new to say, because what is remarkable about all the newspaper coverage is that the same words keep leaping out from different pages - decency, integrity, trust, dignity, scholar, service and commitment.

Tributes have been coming in from all manner of people. He visited the Irish Parliament a few months ago. Its Presiding Officer wrote to me: "Having paid tribute to the integrity and proficiency of such a fine politician, the members of the Dáil rose in prayerful silence."

In May, we had a visit from the President of Malawi. Donald's heart trouble had already been diagnosed and he had cancelled most of his engagements prior to his operation. However, he was due to give a dinner in Edinburgh Castle for the President and he told me: "That is one I am going to keep". He not only gave the dinner, but he spent the evening showing the President round the castle and over the Honours of Scotland, revelling in expounding our history and discussing Scotland's links with Africa through David Livingstone and others.

On Wednesday evening, within hours of the tragic news, I was astonished to receive a telephone call from the President of Malawi himself, expressing his sadness and conveying his condolences to the Parliament. Those two tributes show how Donald touched and impressed those whom he had met but fleetingly. How much more painful, therefore, is his loss to those who knew him well.

However, tributes have come not just from the great and the powerful, but from every walk of life. One Scottish organisation wrote:

"While we and he had not seen eye to eye on every aspect of policy, it had been a comfort to know that the Executive was headed by a man who personified the highest possible standards in public life."

I add the words of two typical individuals, which I have chosen at random. One said that he "was not a supporter of his party but, like many others, knew him to be a great ambassador for Scotland and a genuinely good man." Another stated "Yesterday should have been a day of celebration for me - it was my 40th birthday. I had never met the man, but when I heard the news of his death, I simply had no stomach for a party."

Furthermore, one entry in our condolence book contains, alongside the signature, just one word: "Thankyou". That is what we come together today to say.

However, Donald would not forgive us if we turned this into a greetin' meeting, because there was one other characteristic of Donald's that I have not yet mentioned - he was always enormous fun to be with. I am going to miss our tete-a-tete dinners dreadfully.

Let me tell you about two episodes with Donald, which both - like all good Donald stories - involve food. More than 40 years ago, a group of Scottish university students visited the Soviet Union. Donald was one, I was another and the Deputy Presiding Officer, George Reid, was also there. We spent a week in Moscow and a week in Leningrad, and the food - especially student food - was of disgustingly poor quality; indeed, a few of us, including Donald, were quite ill.

On our arrival in Kiev for the third week, we sat down to lunch. Suddenly, plates of cream buns appeared and Donald more or less led a standing ovation. He inquired hopefully whether, by any chance, any of the rest of us did not like cream buns and generally displayed such excessive enthusiasm that, to his delight, our host produced cream buns again for dinner. He also produced them for breakfast the next morning, and again at lunch, and for every single meal during that week. I blame Donald for the fact that I have never since then been able to face a cream bun.

On Monday evening, the night before he died, I formally opened the new visitors centre at Holyrood. I spoke of the progress on our new building and of the importance of public access to its development. I paid tribute to architect Enric Miralles, whose widow was with us. I had just finished my speech when Donald shambled into the room. I had not been expecting him and mockingly scolded him saying: "You've just missed the best part of the evening". With a withering look, he said: "Your speech? Oh, I don't think so. These look like excellent canapès." He added: "As a matter of fact, David, I think I have just demonstrated for you yet again my impeccable sense of judgement and timing."

Donald Dewar elevated the profession of politician. As an occupation, politics is too easily derided, but to be a politician should be the highest and noblest calling of all - involvement in the responsible and accountable governance of people's lives. In a television interview about a decade ago, Lord Hailsham said:

"Nobody I think who knows enough about politics really wants to be a leader. Only a fool would want to stand in that position when you are exposed to the whims of fortune and chance and all the rest of it."

I do not agree. Of course leadership involves taking knocks and Donald had his share, both personal and political. However, it also provides an opportunity to point a course, to stamp a platform and to gather others to one's cause - Donald used his qualities of leadership to do all of those.

Now that he is gone, where does that leave us? I commend to you lines by Archbishop Darbyshire, who wrote:

> *"Not names engraved in marble make*
> *The best memorials of the dead;*
> *But burdens shouldered for their sake*
> *And tasks completed in their stead."*

All of us in the chamber have tasks to complete in his stead.

# The Rt.hon JIM WALLACE MSP
*Deputy First Minister, Minister for Justice and Leader of the Scottish Liberal Democrats*

Today we meet as a Parliament that is tragically bereft. Indeed, Scotland is a nation bereft. We have reconvened to express our deep shock at the sudden and oh, so untimely death of our First Minister, Donald Dewar.

We meet to pay tribute to a great leader, an outstanding parliamentarian, a colleague and a friend. Put simply, Donald was a fundamentally honest and decent man. He was also a loyal man. He was loyal to his friends, to his colleagues and to the Labour party - the party that he not only led, but to which he devoted his life. Above all, he was loyal to Scotland.

Our grief and sense of loss is shared by millions who never met him or knew him. However, the thoughts and most heartfelt sympathy of all of us in the Parliament go to his closest friends and to those who loved him most - Marion and Ian.

I met Donald first about 20 years ago in a Glasgow sheriff court, but I hasten to add that we were both there in a professional capacity. Later, we became friends, even although we were political opponents most of the time. However, recently I had the privilege of working with Donald in Government. Ours was a partnership that was based not only on a written agreement, but on trust. Donald Dewar was a man whom people could trust. His parliamentary skills were legendary, although wonderfully expressive phrases such as "Get down on your hunkers", delivered in his typical quick-fire manner, must have created consternation among the Hansard reporters.

Donald relished the cut and thrust of political debate, but what he relished most was doing things - achieving things, turning political words into political action and making a difference for people, most of all here in Scotland.

Donald Dewar loved Scotland. He loved Scotland's places, Scotland's art, Scotland's culture, Scotland's history and even Scotland's football. Most important, he loved Scotland's people and spent a lifetime in politics fighting for a fairer and more socially just nation. Each of us will have heard him argue with passion that his constituents in one of our country's most deprived areas should enjoy the same opportunities, the same life chances and the same life expectancy as those who live in Scotland's more affluent communities.

If Donald loved Scotland's people, the tributes from across the land have shown just how much the people loved and revered him. It is difficult enough for a politician to earn respect, but it requires a very special person to earn respect and win affection. Donald Dewar was a man who, through a lifetime of tireless political service, showed that our profession of politics can be a noble calling.

In one respect, for Donald the opening of our Parliament was the culmination of years of dedicated and sustained endeavour: the bitter disappointments of 1979; the long years in Opposition; the hope that was rekindled by the constitutional convention; the scale of the referendum victory; the delivery of the Scotland Act 1998; the establishment of this Parliament; and the historic achievement of becoming our first First Minister. For Donald, however, the creation of our Parliament was not enough. In the memorable speech that he delivered in the chamber on 1 July last year he said:

> *"A Scottish Parliament. Not an end: a means to greater ends."*

He looked forward to the days "when this Chamber will sound with debate, argument and passion. When men and women from all over Scotland will meet to work together for a future built from the first principles of social justice."

Therefore, how fitting it is that we pay tribute to Donald Dewar today in The Scottish Parliament - the Parliament for which he campaigned, the Parliament that he delivered and the Parliament that he led.

As leader of the Scottish Liberal Democrats, I want to share a quote from the great Liberal Prime Minister, W E Gladstone, although I know that had Donald still been with us, he would have rolled his eyes to the ceiling at this point and come out with a witty and well-honed put-down. However, Donald had a keen sense of political history, so I have decided to share the quote anyway.

In a speech that he gave in the Dalkeith Corn Exchange in November 1879, William Gladstone said:

> *"The man who shall devise a machinery by which some portion of the excessive and impossible task now laid upon the House of Commons shall be shifted to the more free and therefore more efficient hands of devolved authorities, will confer a blessing upon his country that will entitle him to be reckoned among the prominent benefactors of the land."*

Donald Dewar was the man who devised and delivered such machinery.

This Parliament is his legacy, not only to the Scotland of today, but to future generations of Scots. Our most real and lasting tribute to Donald Dewar will be to secure the Parliament's success and, through that, to build a nation of which he would have been proud.

We will miss him terribly.

# MR JOHN SWINNEY MSP

*Leader of The Scottish National Party*


I wish to express the sadness of the Scottish National Party at the death of Donald Dewar and to extend our sympathy to Marion and Ian Dewar, to Donald's many friends and to all those who worked alongside him in the Executive, in the Labour Party, in the civil service and in The Scottish Parliament. We have all lost a fine colleague.

These have been difficult days for everyone in Scotland - unimaginably difficult days for those who were closest to Donald Dewar. We all pray that in the days ahead, everyone who has been affected by the death of our First Minister will find comfort and peace.

I speak today after only three weeks as Donald Dewar's opposite number, but I speak on behalf of all my colleagues who enjoyed co-operation - and conflict - with Donald over many years. Donald was a man whose legacy we see around us: he was a man who changed a nation for the better. What greater tribute can there be?

This Parliament is our nation's Parliament. It was crafted by the skills and energies of many people. Donald Dewar talked about those people - some of whom did not live long enough to see our Parliament - on July 1 last year when he stated:

"Today, we reach back through the long haul to win this Parliament, through the struggles of those who brought democracy to Scotland".

He was talking about others, but today I am talking about him.

Donald Dewar was a man who supported devolution when it was in fashion and when it was out of fashion. To the exasperation of his spin-doctors, but to the delight of the people, being in fashion never seemed to fash Donald Dewar.

We heard a poem about Scotland by Iain Crichton Smith on the Parliament's opening day. He called on our country to be:

> *"True to itself and to its origins,*
> *Inventive, original, philosophical".*

Donald Dewar was a man who was true to himself and to his origins. The Scotland Act 1998, which he delivered, was an inventive and original piece of legislation. He devoted his energies and intellect to crafting - through many battles, I am sure - legislation that has given clarity to our Scottish Parliament.

Donald Dewar never saw The Scottish Parliament as an end in itself, but as the means to transform the lives of the people of our country - today I salute him for that.

Donald had a habit of often expressing the grandest of comments in a downbeat or matter of fact way - perhaps even using massive understatement. He opened his last major speech, which he delivered on 29 September in Dublin, with these words:

"Political dialogue is not always easy in my country".

Well, we can all think of moments that showed that he had a point, but we can also think of times when political dialogue has worked and when Donald Dewar ensured that that was the case.

I think particularly of the 1997 referendum campaign. After a bruising election, Donald went out of his way - in the language that he used, in the style that he deployed and in the dialogue that he undertook - to ensure that we in the Scottish National Party, with our different yet complementary agenda, could play our part in delivering the devolved Parliament. The mechanism that he used for that purpose - the pledge that he gave to that end - was a plain recognition that the people who live in this country have the ability to determine their own future.

Donald captured that sense again in his speech to Parliament on 1 July 1999, when he stated:

"For me, for any Scot, today is a proud moment; a new stage on a journey begun long ago and which has no end."

For all that we had - still have - different visions of our final destination, Donald Dewar saw that we all agreed that the journey had to begin. He made sure that it did. Donald Dewar was able on that and other occasions to reach beyond his party interest to speak to and for the whole of Scotland.

One strong voice has gone, but its echo will remain; its message will continue in all our voices, determined to make this Parliament a success and determined to win the precious social justice that Donald Dewar sought in his political life.

In the past few days, many people, including a number of people in the SNP, have spoken of the immense loyalty and affection that Donald Dewar generated in those who worked closely with him. I am told that civil servants referred to him not only respectfully as the First Minister, but as "the boss". He led and was part of a team. To build, motivate and hold the genuine affection of such a team shows the very special combination of qualities that were held by our late First Minister.

In conclusion I will refer for the last time to some words that were used by Donald Dewar when he addressed Parliament at its state opening. It is a speech to which I have referred frequently, because it was a most beautiful speech. Donald talked of the four words that are woven into the symbolic thistles on our mace. Those four words are wisdom, justice, compassion and integrity. Those are words that we should live up to in the Parliament - they are our founding principles.

Today, we reflect on the sad loss of our First Minister; the loss of a towering figure in Scottish politics and the loss of a father and a grandfather. For some, that loss is the loss of a friend. For some it is the loss of a colleague and for others, it is the loss of an adversary. For us all, it is the loss of a fellow Scots parliamentarian.

We can hold firm to the words on our mace. We can say truly of Donald Dewar that, in his life, he offered wisdom, justice, compassion and integrity. In his memory, we in the Parliament should live up to those words.

# MR DAVID McLETCHIE MSP
*Leader of the Scottish Conservative and Unionist Party*

Any tribute to Donald Dewar must recognise his enormous contribution to Scottish political life, but it is equally, if not more, important to recognise his qualities as a man. The regard in which he is held by Scots from all walks of life is recognition not only of his political talents and achievements, but of the way in which he conducted himself in public life. He was a towering figure - literally and metaphorically.

One does not have to be of the same political persuasion as another to recognise in them someone who has ability, sincerity and conviction. Donald Dewar was committed to serving his fellow Scots and to improving the lives of everyone in our country. It is a goal that we all share, even if we may differ on what the means should be.

The creation of a Scottish Parliament was central to the achievement of his goal. It was for him, as we all know, a very personal crusade. As opponents of the proposals, we in the Conservative party know only too well that no one did more than Donald Dewar to advance that case with rational argument and passion, which was founded on his conviction that it was the right course for Scotland. By delivering overwhelming majorities in the referendum, he put devolution beyond doubt. That has changed the political landscape forever for all of us and not least for those in my party.

Once the dust of the election battle had settled, his appointment as the first First Minister of The Scottish Parliament was a foregone but fitting conclusion. It was a post made for him and made by him.

Sadly, his time as First Minister has been cut short, but his place in the history books is assured. To attain high office in politics is a long climb to the top of a greasy pole. However, to hold high office with distinction requires greater qualities and virtues. It is widely recognised that Donald Dewar had those qualities and virtues in abundance. He was a man who combined many of the traditional virtues that we admire in our fellow citizens - honesty, decency, integrity, industry and self-sacrifice. He brought those qualities and virtues to this most modern of parliaments.

My acquaintance with Donald Dewar was short compared with that of many of the others who have paid tribute to him in recent days, because I am one of the 105 members of The Scottish Parliament who have not previously been a member of any parliament. However, as one of the new boys, I appreciated Donald's unfailing courtesy towards opponents and his sense of propriety, which brought dignity to our proceedings. Donald Dewar set the standard for Scotland's Parliament - a standard to which we can all aspire, even if few of us will equal it.

As I know from my regular jousts with Donald at question time, he was a man who relished debate and possessed great intellect, erudition and a sharp wit. In the modern vernacular, he would be described as a class act. As many people have pointed out, Donald Dewar was a politician who had a wide range of interests - art, history and literature. He brought a width of knowledge and learning to the chamber, with which he enriched our debates.

We all have personal memories of him. I recall a question time last April when he commented that I had a "pawky manner", which "occasionally suggests something from Trollope."

As I sat in my seat thinking of a response, I knew only two things. First, it was Anthony and not Joanna Trollope that he was talking about. Secondly, if Donald Dewar said that one was like a character from a Trollope novel, it was a judgement that it would be pointless to contest.

We were all deeply shocked and saddened by the death of Donald Dewar, none more so than his close colleagues who worked with him from day to day. On Tuesday and Wednesday of this week, it fell to his adviser, David Whitton, to undertake the distressing and unenviable task of reporting to the country on the First Minister's condition. I would like to place on record our admiration for the moving and professional manner in which David Whitton discharged that role.

However, our greatest sympathies are reserved for Donald Dewar's family and all our thoughts are with them at this time. I hope that in the days and weeks ahead, knowledge of the country's deep respect, regard and affection for Donald Dewar will bring them comfort and strength. They can take pride in the fact that, by his life and work, he will be remembered as a Scotsman for all seasons.

# The Rt.hon HENRY McLEISH MSP
*Scottish Labour Party*

When Donald Dewar walked into this Parliament 15 months ago, as First Minister at the first meeting of the first Scottish Parliament, he spoke not only as the architect of Scottish devolution, but as the advocate for what had shaped his lifetime of service - social justice.

We all think of Donald not simply as a parliamentary colleague, but as a friend. We do not bear the full impact of this tragedy, unlike Donald's family - Marion and Ian - and his close friends, but we feel their loss and we are thinking about them today.

As a nation, here in our new Parliament we mourn together the loss of Donald. Today, in our grief, we speak for the whole Scottish nation, giving voice to the feelings of all the communities that we represent.

In an age of cynicism about politicians, to the people of Scotland, Donald was never "one of them" - he was always "one of us". He had no pretence and no pomposity. He was a man of the people and he was close to the people - a man whom people felt they knew before they met him. There was no title of which he was prouder than the one that he shared with every one of us: member of The Scottish Parliament. Donald Dewar was a man who sought that position for what he could do, not for what he would be.

Donald's life was rooted in Glasgow. To him, his first and foremost responsibility was to his constituents, whom he served with dedication and pride. He thought of his duty to others first and of his personal welfare last. It is no surprise to those of us who knew him well that, even while he was desperately ill only three days ago, he was determined to get on with the job and do his duty. He was more worried about inconveniencing anybody else than he was about his health. He even apologised for causing a fuss. He was courageous, selfless, kind and concerned for others to the last.

Donald also had faith in his nation and he truly embraced the soul of Scotland. He was a cultured man - an expert on literature, the arts, poetry and sport and a collector of books and paintings. Let us remind ourselves of the brilliant and moving speech that he made at the opening of Parliament last July. Donald said:

"This is about more than our politics and our laws. This is about who we are, how we carry ourselves. In the quiet moments today, we might hear some echoes from the past.

The shout of the welder in the din of the great Clyde shipyards; the speak of the Mearns, with its soul in the land; the discourse of the enlightenment, when Edinburgh and Glasgow were a light held to the intellectual life of Europe; the wild cry of the Great Pipes; and back to the distant cries of the battles of Bruce and Wallace."

He concluded by saying:

"The past is part of us. But today there is a new voice in the land, the voice of a democratic Parliament. A voice to shape Scotland, a voice for the future."

Over many years, many have championed the cause of devolution. We all know that, in debates and in discussions in the Scottish Grand Committee and the Scottish Constitutional Convention, Donald Dewar did more than anybody to make devolution happen. He, more than any one, won the referendum, because the Scottish people trusted him to make it work. With his unique parliamentary skills, he drove the Scotland Act 1998 through the Westminster Parliament. In 1999, people put their faith in him because they knew that he was on their side and, of course, as our leader, he has steered us through our Parliament's first year.

Many stories have been told about Donald Dewar in recent days and I want to contribute to that and illustrate how self-effacing Donald was and how he was a man of great achievement who never blew his own trumpet.

In the early days after 1997, the fleshing out of the details of the devolution white paper in Westminster involved Donald in day-to-day combat with some of the biggest political beasts in the Westminster jungle. Invariably, he would come back to Dover House exasperated and gloomy about his performance and, of course, suffering fools gladly was never one of Donald's strongest suits. I became slightly concerned about that daily ritual and so I decided to speak to the Scottish civil servants who had been with him to find out what was happening. As I suspected, Donald had on every occasion won hands down. That intellectual and physical stamina produced the basis of where we are today. That is a poignant message for me, because it was part of the task of winning devolution for Scotland.

Today Parliament gathers united in grief. We all mourn, but we on the Labour benches mourn for one of our own.

Throughout his lifetime of service, in Edinburgh, at Westminster and in his years of service in his constituency, Donald fought for devolution and social justice. He was unshakeable in his opposition to poverty and held the simple conviction that all should have an equal chance. He put those causes first.

His ambition was not for the Parliament of Scotland but for the people of Scotland. He believed that everyone was of equal worth and that all should have an equal chance. That is why he treated everyone equally. It is those principles that will serve as a guide to us all in the days that lie ahead.

Speaking only a few weeks ago, Donald said:

"We will hold to our principles. Top of the list is the attack upon poverty, the drive to create opportunity . . . the vision of a just society."

His intellect, his good humour, his unsurpassed debating skills and his integrity have graced this Parliament. More than that, his vision now challenges this Parliament. With devolution, he turned a dream into a promise and a commitment into a reality, in this building.

Colleagues, we have lost the most powerful voice for that dream, but Donald has left his vision, his values and the hopes that they awakened. We are now the trustees of that dream. It falls to all of us to ensure that his dream, his promise and his commitment to a socially just community can also become a reality in the chamber and in Scotland. Let us commit ourselves to that today.

All of us will remember the last time we saw him - each of us has our own private memories and personal experiences of a life that was so tragically cut short.

Donald Dewar - 1937 to 2000 - now takes his special place on the list of Scotland's favourite sons. Donald the person, the politician and the patriot gave us a unique record of public service and his greatest achievement was devolution - a great life and a great legacy.

*"With thanks from the future generations of Scots"*

(Source: Scottish Parliament Condolence Book)

# Donald Dewar's Funeral

On October 18, Scotland paid its last farewells to the first First Minister with his funeral in Glasgow Cathedral.

In a simple but dignified ceremony, mourners from all walks of life - from The Prince of Wales to schoolchildren, party leaders to canteen staff - were joined by thousands lining the streets of Glasgow and watching on TV as moving tributes were paid to Donald Dewar.

The two main tributes came from Chancellor Gordon Brown and writer and broadcaster Ruth Wishart.

# The Rt.hon GORDON BROWN MP
*Chancellor of the Exchequer*

Donald Dewar would have been the last to acknowledge the true scale of his life's achievements. But the friend we lost only seven days ago was one of only a handful of people across the centuries of whom it could be said: "He founded a new parliament."

Over decades, and with a matchless constancy of purpose, he more than anyone fashioned Scotland's old democratic instincts into the modern democratic institution. And all of us privileged to work under his leadership know that in doing so he changed both Scotland and Britain irreversibly and for the better.

People will ask, as they have done over the last week, why, with such achievements to his name, why, with such a breadth of friendship and a hinterland of such continental proportions, why did he go on, even in ill health, why did he continue to work, and work himself so hard?
He went on because he felt his work was not yet done. For him, constitutional reform was not an end in itself but the means to an even greater end - social justice - so he went back to work.

"We cannot accept a Scotland," he said, launching the Parliament's first legislative programme, "where 4,000 children leave school each year without qualifications, where a third of Scottish households are below the average UK income, where a quarter of our housing stock suffers from dampness. We can use the power of Government to connect, persuade, cajole, encourage, preach, and lead to change that. We can and we shall." And he did.

Because what motivated Donald all through his political life was his own simple and unshakeable belief that poverty was wrong. Donald refused to accept that the people of Drumchapel, or of any community, should have diminished dreams or lesser lives simply because of where they were born.

"No child should be born to fail", he said, and he never wavered.

Even when he lost in Aberdeen, as Labour lost in 1970, when he could have retreated into the comfortable life of a solicitor, he chose instead to make Scotland's Children's Panel system work in one of our poorest communities to help young people in trouble.

Then back in Parliament in 1978, moved by the plight of people who needed him. The hundreds of meetings, the thousands of letters, meticulously written, always there to serve. The MP for Garscadden, latterly MSP for Anniesland, the only titles he really cherished.

Everyone knew someone Donald had helped and from these innumerable encounters he gained strength for the larger battles.

And through 18 years of Opposition, as he moved from Shadow Scottish then Social Security Secretary to Chief Whip, always a committed European, even when it was unfashionable, and then to the Cabinet, he used his unquestioned mastery of the debating chamber of the House of Commons, easy for him after the real thing at Glasgow University Union.

He used this mastery to speak up consistently for his causes - education, the health service, the needs of the elderly, and against the poll tax and, all illiberal laws, he always stood firm.

Everyone here today will remember when first they met or talked with Donald Dewar. I first had a conversation with him only yards from here as a young student in 1972 on the Great Upper Clyde shipbuilders' Right to Work march and sometime later, when I felt fortunate and pleased to be joining him, elected for the first first time to our party's Scottish Executive.

I said: "I look forward to the first meeting." "I can assure you," he said with his characteristic directness, "that it will be awful"!

But what he was marching for in 1972, only a few yards from here, he was still working for in his final days. In our last conversation together, just as in our first, he was making the case for work for the Clyde. Such constancy of commitment, one of so many reasons why in a nation united in mourning, the Labour Party he loved grieved so much for the loss of one of our own.

So when people say: "What was special about Donald was his decency", they tell you far less than half the story. What was special about Donald as a politician, was that consistently, and tirelessly, he pursued the logic of his decency and worked for a just and more equal society.

Donald's achievements explained the great respect in which he was held, unusual for a politician. But how do we explain the even greater affection for him, something almost unique in political life?

People trusted him. And why?

He said himself that as the only son of elderly parents, often too ill to care for him, and sent to boarding school very young, his school days were bookish and often lonely.

But Glasgow University let Donald flourish. As part of a remarkable collection of friendships that lasted an entire lifetime. A circle that sustained him through political and personal adversity. From then on, wherever he worked, Glasgow was home. Not just its architecture, book-shops, galleries and curry houses, but because he was at home with the people.

Glasgow's directness, its welcoming warmth, its deflating wit, its humane irreverence and above all its uniquely egalitarian sense of itself. And no-one came to embody that egalitarian spirit better than Donald. Always true to himself. Wherever he was and whoever he was with. And so many of us witnessed at first hand in his Garscadden election in 1978 and in all parts of the country ever since, the unique political chemistry he created around him, and it was never because he told people just what they wanted to hear.

Rain, sleet or snow, in all seasons, Donald emerging from a battered old car, that always seemed smaller than himself. It's back seat strewn with leaflets from the last campaign - and the one before that. His towering frame a size and shape Marks and Spencers had never thought of. Donald striding out and engaging with people. His old fashioned courtesy "Good morning, indeed". His ready laugh. His sometime breathtaking directness: "Madam, what an extraordinary hat - Kylie, what a preposterous name".

And perhaps only a few paces on, or later over a plate of scones, little scenes from the day would reappear as marvellous, mischievous, sometimes merciless anecdotes, afterwards to be recounted anywhere from the MP's tearoom to the pensioner's lunchclub, or a friends dinner table with the verve and timing of the best of Scotland's stand-up comics.

The life-enhancing Donald, full of wit, yet scholarly and erudite.

The biography he always planned to write was of the churchman and reformer Thomas Chalmers. The work he often dipped into most was Gladstone's Diaries.

Donald - endlessly charismatic but always modest. A constant friend, and the first you would think of to invite to a party.

All of us have stories about Donald. But all of us know that all of them could have been told much better by Donald himself.

And so we can understand why, in an age when people often cross the street to avoid a politician, people would cross the street to meet and to talk to Donald, and why he was, for so many people, across Scotland, not First Minister, but more than that - simply Donald.

Perhaps the common thread that runs through this extraordinary life that we celebrate today, is that Donald reached out to people, and in turn people reached out to him and trusted him. Because he honoured their individuality, their needs, their strengths, their potential, and even their eccentricities, so many of them honoured him and his. They saw him as one of their own. A friend who stood with them.

This was Donald's gift. To establish not only a unique bond of trust with people, but also a common cause with them. People came to believe not only in what he did but what he stood for. The cause of social justice. The rock on which his lifetime of public service was built.

Donald's achievement is much more than a Parliament. Much more than the sum of his social reforms. It is that he ennobled the very idea of service and by his pursuit of a just society, he gave moral purpose to our public life.

Donald was a great man, but he was better than that. He was a great man and a good man. A man of great integrity and of high ideas, who having earned the people's trust was faithful unto the last and delivered for us mighty achievements that will endure long after we are gone. Let us all, friends, colleagues, give thanks for a life of service and say to each other:

"His ideals, this life, Donald Dewar's vision of a just society, now challenge us. Though he is gone from us his cause endures, so let us re-dedicate ourselves to his ideals and to the work he has left for us. Let his inspiration now lead us forward."

# RUTH WISHART
*Writer and broadcaster*

I have the daunting privilege to speak today on behalf of Donald's private army: his friends.

And if there is one tiny crumb of comfort in the knowledge that he is absent from this huge gathering of family, friends and colleagues, it is that for the first time it will be possible to pay tribute *to him* without being heckled *by him*.

From which you may gather that being able to count Donald Campbell Dewar as a friend was not an unalloyed blessing.

Share with him your holiday plans and he would guffaw with derision at your proposed destination.

This from a man who, for many of his adult years, did not possess a valid passport. He had a suspicion, he said, that travel might narrow his mind.

Invite him to dinner and he would tuck heartily into the reputations of his fellow guests before relieving them of the remnants of their pudding.

Attend the theatre in his company and you risked his giving a running commentary on the paucity of the production values. These remarks generally fell some way short of being *sotto voce*.

All this was tolerated by his friends because in return for coping with his social idiosyncrasies you were privileged to enjoy his wonderful wit, benefit from his erudition and have the comforting knowledge that this man would be a foul weather friend. With Donald, loyalty was always a two way street.

Many thousands of words have been written about him over the last few difficult days. And the obituary writers have had no shortage of hinterland to explore. His love of literature has been well documented. His tastes were catholic, not to say esoteric.

Last year the Edinburgh International Book Festival contrived an event where I was to interview Donald about six books which had a seminal influence on his thinking. As the day drew near, the Festival called to say that he had still not been in touch with the relevant list - could I perhaps chivvy him a little since they wanted to be sure to have extra sales copies available of those volumes given the First Minister's public seal of approval.

I called Donald and he read over the titles and authors he planned to include.

It was difficult going back to the Festival Director with the dispiriting news that none of them was still in print!

The visual arts were an enduring passion. One of his most pleasurable pieces of recent business was opening an exhibition of The Scottish Colourists in Kirkcudbright.

His love of sport is legendary. His knowledge of football in particular was extensive. This was a man who could bore for Scotland on the relative merits of 3-5-2 versus 4-3-3 and not infrequently did.

I last spoke with him on Saturday the 7th of October. Tragic news had just reached us that in the last international to be held at Wembley, Germany had defeated England one-nil in a World Cup qualifying tie.

He bore it bravely!

There have been less than flattering references to his sartorial style. Many people have suggested he did not appear to own an overcoat.

This was a foul calumny. As the archive footage of the Garscadden by-election decisively demonstrated, he did indeed have an outer garment. Its passing was not much mourned by the world of fashion ...

One summer evening, just after he became Secretary of State for Scotland, we agreed to meet for supper in celebration of his realising a long cherished ambition.

Gallus Glasgow was decked out in summer shorts and halter tops. Donald arrived in a suit complete with pullover. His solitary concession to the temperature was a pair of sandshoes of less than recent vintage. He had bought them some years before, it transpired, because he had been invited to join John Smith and his family on holiday in rural France.

I rather fear these 'sannies' represented his entire holiday wardrobe.

At one lunch he sported a tie with a YSL motif. A breakthrough, I surmised. Yves St Laurent had persuaded him of the merits of designer chic. Not at all, he retorted. He had been presented with it - by Yarrow Shipbuilders Ltd!

His elevation to First Minister and the presence of young women in his cabinet finally convinced him that owning more than two suits would not be considered unduly decadent.

It also ensured that when he had an audience with Her Majesty at Holyrood Palace there would be a higher probability of matching socks.

He was, in every bone and sinew, a Glasgow man.

I mean no slight to Scotland's magnificent capital when I say that Donald's spirits visibly lifted at that portion of the M8 where the skyline of his native city first becomes visible.

People have talked of Donald Dewar as a solitary man. That is not so. Rather he was a man who cherished the rare bonus of solitude.

The fact of his illness last May afforded him unsolicited leisure which, typically, he thought he might use to acquire new skills. A sleek laptop computer arrived from his office and he showed it off with all the wide eyed enthusiasm of a boy acquiring his first train set. I never saw either the computer lid or the instruction manual in the open position.

Importantly that period gave him more quality time with Marion and Ian whom he loved dearly and of whom he was enormously proud. Ian's daughter Hazel, born in January 1999, is the only woman he honoured with a picture at his bedside. His children bear the greatest burden today.

But they bear it in the knowledge that their father was a great Scot ... and a very fine human being.

# WORDS OF WISDOM

## *Donald Dewar's speeches*

Politicians make hundreds of speeches throughout their career. Donald Dewar was no exception. A great deal of thought and preparation went into his addresses, no matter the subject, regardless of the audience.

His ability to hold a gathering in thrall was testimony to his undoubted speaking ability, honed at Glasgow University and perfected in the Parliamentary Chambers in London and Edinburgh.

Any attempt to select 'the best' of Donald Dewar's speeches would be futile and foolish. What we reproduce here are three of his most thought-provoking addresses from the post-devolution period.

# THE SCOTTISH PARLIAMENT: THE CHALLENGES AHEAD

*St Andrews - 30 November 1998*
*(The Scotland Bill received Royal Assent less than two weeks earlier on November 19)*

I am grateful to St Andrews and Fife - town, gown and Kingdom - for inviting me here this St Andrew's Day.

And I am grateful to St Andrew himself for being able to speak at all. St Andrew is the patron saint of those with sore throats, and I am one among them. He is also the patron saint of singers, fishmongers, those with gout and women who wish to become mothers. I resist the temptation to find the hidden link.

One other word about St Andrew himself. Those who know their hagiography will tell you that he was tied, not nailed, to his cross. This was to prolong his suffering. His persecutors got more than they bargained for. He preached to the mob for two hours before he died.

I am inspired to ask if you are sitting comfortably.

On St Andrew's Day, I want to talk about The Scottish Parliament and the challenges ahead.

The Scotland Act is now law. By St Andrew's Day next, we will have a Scottish Parliament and Scottish Executive.

We have come a long way in the last 18 months. A Scottish Parliament is at last in sight. To achieve that, we had to set a cracking pace.

We said that we would hold a referendum on devolution by the autumn of 1997. We did.

We said that we would introduce legislation to enact our devolution proposals within a year of coming to office. We did. And now that legislation is law.

We press on. Much remains to be done, practical arrangements to get the Parliament in place. The pace is fast. But we know where we're going.

St Andrew's Day is an opportunity to pause, to think, to look ahead. We are bringing into existence a Parliament with a wide range of powers, with great authority over the affairs of Scotland.

What will be the big challenges before it? What opportunities should it seek out to better the lives of the people of Scotland?

Scotland has had a remarkable history. The union of 1707 was a merger not a take-over. There were guarantees. Our law, our religion and our administrative systems would be protected. Those guarantees have been honoured.

The historian Linda Colley has argued that the justification for the Union died with the years. Scotland and England were pressed together by necessity, not affection. The necessities which drove politics in the 18th and early 19th century have, it is true, faded. No one now is desperate to shut the back door against France or to secure the Protestant succession, though the Scottish imperative of gaining access to English markets still has resonance. But if at the end of the first quarter of the nineteenth century the old imperatives died, new ones took their place and Scotland prospered mightily from the Empire and its trade.

In Scotland, the 19th century was the period of North British railways and North British hotels and more fundamentally the aping of polite London society. A threat to Scottishness?

Lord Cockburn thought so. The great recorder of nineteenth century Edinburgh life, a man who would have ranked with Pepys had he lived in London, lamented in the 1850s that by the end of the century Scotland would be "but an English county".

Cockburn was a cultural nationalist, a man as keen on preserving the difference that was the Scotland of his day as he was to pilot reform on a British basis. He and Jeffrey should never be forgotten. They piloted the Great Reform Bill, Scottish version. Their enthusiasm led Jeffrey to found the Edinburgh Review - the house magazine of the Enlightenment in the late eighteenth century. Cockburn feared that

*"Nothing can prevent the gradual disappearance of local manners and their absorption [and] assimilation by a far larger, richer and more powerful kindred and adjoining kingdom."*

*"Burns and Scott have done more for the preservation of proper Scotland than could ever be accomplished by law, statesmen or associations. How can we retain our language respectably after it has become vulgar in the ear of our native gentility: after scarcely a single Scotch nobleman will keep a house in a Scotch town: and after our soil and especially our Highlands are passing rapidly into English hands? This is all very sad but it is the natural course: and foolish associations with their nonsense about Bannockburn and the Union only hasten the progress by bringing the taste for averting it into discredit."*

It all sounds painfully familiar, but of course Cockburn was wrong. Scotland was already building the cultural platform which stands today.

Cockburn was a link between the age of Hume, Hutchinson, Dougald Stewart, Principal Robertson and the high days of the Victorian industrial revolution. At the same time he looked to Burns, Fergusson and Alan Ramsay the Elder to revive and build the continuity that reinforced and blended with the great European traditions that had inspired the Enlightenment.

Cockburn's pessimism was not justified. Scottish confidence grew and with it a feeling of a need for a new deal. It was not essentially a political feeling. No one would accuse Campbell Bannerman of being a nationalist when in 1885 - the year in which the Scottish Office was founded - he changed his address from 'Belmont Castle, Meigle, NB' - North Britain - to 'Belmont Castle, Meigle, Scotland'.

It was not linguistic. The Scots language and Gaelic are part of Scottishness, but national identity in Scotland is not a linguistic identity, as it is to a greater degree in Catalonia, in Quebec.

The demand for a new deal for Scotland was built upon a genuine sense of cultural identity. There was a feeling that dual nationality mattered. As John McIntosh argued 20 years ago, we were then, we are now, both Scots and citizens of the United Kingdom.

A moment's diversion. Checking some quotations for this speech last night, I found a cutting from the Glasgow Herald. It dates from the late sixties and records the founding of a backbencher group 'to press the cause of regional government - including separate parliaments for Scotland and Wales'.

Mr John McIntosh MP was one of the founders. The other two named and shamed in the article were Donald Dewar, MP for South Aberdeen and PPS to Tony Crosland; and Robert McLennan, Labour MP for Caithness and Sutherland.

The founding of the Group was described as a 'deliberate attempt to influence policy with the Government and the Labour Party'. But, you will be glad to know that this nascent lobby was established with the approval of Mr John Silkin, then the Government Chief Whip.

That was thirty years or so ago. The Devolution settlement secures and makes patent the promises of three hundred years ago. It finally secures the institutional structures that have survived with such tenacity and underpinned Scottish life in the period between.

The platform built in the past stands today. In painting, there was the Glasgow School, the superb colourists, Peploe, Cadell and Ferguson. Today, there is a strong, distinct tradition: the late David Donaldson, Goudie, Campbell, Conroy, Alison Watt and many others.

Literature has been lively, with novels good, bad and in between according to taste carrying a strong and distinctive Scottish voice. Poets like Hugh MacDiarmid, Sorley MacLean, Norman MacCaig, Robert Crawford, Douglas Dunn.

There is a live, popular Scottish culture. I tell you so. In a primary school the other day, faced by thirty very new Scots, an instant opinion poll revealed 28 regular readers of the Beano. DC Thomson still rules, despite Tom Nairn's cry that Scotland would never be free until the last Minister was strangled with the last copy of the Sunday Post.

We have a Parliament again. But we are not going back to the future. We have a Parliament again, but not because it makes sense to wrench ourselves out of the merger we entered those centuries ago.

We have a Scottish Parliament because we are Scots and because Scots want to govern their domestic affairs here in Scotland, a nation with an identity. We have a United Kingdom because Scots are partners in a Union to which we have given much and which has brought us much. I believe we are stronger together, weaker apart.

Let me say why.

The changes we are making are profound, profoundly important to the people of Scotland. There is much talk of history in the making. There may be some hyperbole in that. But when a Parliament last sat in Edinburgh close on 300 years ago, history has to be the reference point, history provides the context.

There are great points of principle at issue in our national debate. One stands above the others: the future of our links with the rest of the United Kingdom. Why does that lie at the heart of political debate this St Andrew's Day? Because one of the Parties contesting the field is a Party built on nationalism. A Party whose sole reason for existence is the desire to create a nation state, with all that that implies.

We cannot settle down to a harmonious, almost cosy, debate as though it did not matter which Party was elected. We - you - have a duty to test and try the respective points of view.

Those who want to take us out of the UK will sketch in a sweep of exciting opportunities for a separate Scotland. Understandably they will not dwell on the difficulties and the downside.

We have to ask the hard questions about the impact of independence on Scotland's finances. The consequences not just for the armed forces but for our defence industries. The problems of dismantling common machinery such as pensions and benefits, customs and excise. The implications for Scottish industry and commerce of a separate currency, different regulatory machinery, north and south of the border.

I do not wish to return to the bruising days I remember all too clearly, when senior opponents branded me a traitor and a Quisling. I stand before you today accused of hysterical scare-mongering. I never dreamt my style was so racy. But it is not scare-mongering to press our case in a civilised, but powerful fashion. To do less would be no service to democracy or Scotland.

Expect us to listen to all those who want to make the Parliament work. Expect us to oppose those who would seek to sour the settlement, to dismantle it.

This is not hysteria: this is common sense. We have not worked long and hard for devolution just to stand idly by at the first challenge.

Those who push alternatives - alternatives which I believe would be damaging to Scotland's future - will be pursued through every by-way and back alley to expose the weakness of their case. Those arguments cannot and will not go by default.

The settlement we have created reflects the settled will of the people of Scotland, expressed in election after election and confirmed beyond doubt by the outcome of the referendum last year.

This is a settlement chewed on and chewed over in public and intense debate over the last 30 years and more. We learnt from the lessons of the 1978 Devolution Act. We learnt from the mistakes and contradictions of years in between. We learnt from the deliberations and decisions of the Constitutional Convention.

What we have is a stable settlement. It is stable because it is the right settlement for Scotland, because it reflects what the people of Scotland want. It strikes the balance between the advantages of doing things our way in Scotland and the advantages of working together in the UK.

Stable but not rigid. We are a Government committed to modernisation. It would be absurd to pretend that ours will be the last word on every detail of the constitutional settlement. Indeed, the framework put in place by the Scotland Act explicitly allows for adjustment, to reflect changing circumstances. If, through experience and by consent, we want to adjust the settlement, the machinery is in place.

It is a very different matter to argue for breaking the settlement, and those that do must demonstrate that they command the support of the people. They have failed in the past. I believe they will fail again. That, of course, is for the electorate.

We may not have built for a millennium. We have built for the new Millennium. A Parliament in Scotland, a Parliament with wide powers; this Parliament has the chance - the responsibility - to build a modern Scotland.

Changing our institutions is not enough in itself. We must improve the lot of the people of Scotland. We change our institutions so that they better reflect and deliver our aspirations.

That is what gives me confidence that the devolution settlement will work. It will work because it responds to the strengths of Scotland. What makes our country special is not just our history, the beauty of the land, a unique and vigorous culture.

What makes our country special is the way we have built our fortunes, not through introspection, but through open engagement with a wider world.

What makes our country special is the strength of our values. Our commitment to equality of opportunity and social justice.

It is the values of the people of this country which will give value to the Parliament. It is the values of the people of Scotland, the way we view the world, which will create the opportunities, the challenges, for the Parliament, for the First Minister and his Executive.

Stand back a moment from the day to day argument. Consider The Scottish Parliament in a wider context. Devolution for Scotland is part of the wider process of democratic renewal embarked on by this Government, from incorporation of the European Convention on Human Rights to reform of the House of Lords - the most radical programme of constitutional reform this century.

This modernising agenda for the UK should itself be seen against the backdrop of the evolving international order. The European Union stands on the brink of fundamental change. Economic and Monetary Union is only weeks away. Enlargement to East and Central Europe is in view, promising to bridge at last the divide that has so long disfigured Europe.

Scotland, the UK, Europe and beyond: we are all bound now into a global economy. The relentless increase in international trade and financial flows is evidence enough - even without the recent economic shocks - to remind us that what happens in far away places does matter to us, does matter to our prosperity.

Looked at from this perspective, Scotland might seem like a small place on the edge of Europe. But it is a place which thrives - which has always thrived - in a larger space, in the UK, in Europe, in the global economy.

That is one challenge to The Scottish Parliament. To recognise that the future prosperity of Scotland lies in that larger space. No economy which has turned its back on the wider world has prospered for long. There are no get-out clauses. There can be no retreat into the back room. We aspire to be there with the best; we must compete with the best.

We can and do compete successfully with the best. We have the capacity, the entrepreneurial drive, to find and win markets for our products.

Our long tradition of excellence in science remains strong. Per head of population, and measured by citations in international scientific journals, our scientists are the third most prolific in the world. That research strength is helping to grow new businesses in new sectors like bio-technology, helping to attract cutting edge companies like Cadence Design Systems.

Scotland is known in the world. What other part of Europe of comparable size gets the recognition of Scotland? No advertising campaign in the world could buy us that. It is priceless. And self evidently this international recognition has not depended upon us being a sovereign nation state. We owe it to our global products. We owe it to the Scots who have done business around the world. We owe it to cultural strength, now expressed as powerfully through film and broadcasting as it ever was through book and song.

We do well in the world. But we could do better. No one can deny that. There is still a productivity gap. Our business start-up rate still lags behind the UK and way behind the best in the world. Our firms invest too little in research and development.

This Government is committed to the modernisation of both the British and Scottish economies. Our aim is stability. Long-term interest rates are at their lowest for 35 years. Inflation is on target at 2.5 per-cent and looks set to stay there for some time.

We have set a rigorous fiscal framework, cutting borrowing by £20 billion in our first year and setting rules to ensure that we borrow only to invest.

We have encouraged enterprise and investment by cutting corporation tax to 30 per-cent generally and to 20 per-cent for smaller businesses, and by cutting capital gains tax on business assets to a new long-term effective rate of 10 per-cent.

We hear today calls, particularly from nationalists, for separate interest rates for Scotland within the United Kingdom. But the economic interests of Scotland and the UK do not diverge in any significant way. Indeed, recent trends have been towards convergence.

Our level of personal disposable income per head is almost exactly the same as for the UK as a whole. Our unemployment rates, GDP per head and other basic indicators are nearer the national average than most regions of the UK.

It is a very odd call when those advocating a separate currency and separate interest rates promise a smooth entry into EMU under which interest rates for Scotland would be set not on a British but on a European basis.

We are proud of our distinctive education system, and rightly so. Education is important, not just for itself but as part of the economic campaign. We made it our top priority, it remains our top priority. We have committed an additional £1.3 billion to Scottish education over the next three years.

It starts with the very youngest children. We have given a commitment to a pre-school education place for all 3-year-olds by 2002.

It goes on into primary education. We have said that we will recruit 5,000 class-room assistants by 2002.

It includes every primary and secondary school in new targets to raise standards. It connects all schools, colleges, universities and libraries in the National Grid for Learning. It means investment in school buildings - £185 million of extra public resources and grant support for private finance initiatives worth £330 million for over 70 schools.

It means a higher level of attainment. We have provided funding to create an additional 42,000 student places in further and higher education. We have set aside £22 million to create 100,000 Individual Learning Accounts to help adults to develop their skills. We are setting up the Scottish University for Industry to make sure that Scottish education can provide what Scottish business needs.

Our people are our potential. We lose the potential of those who can work and who want to work but cannot get work. The New Deal is breaking down the obstacles, and it is working: 3,500 young unemployed Scots into work by the end of September this year.

The Scottish Parliament and Executive will have the opportunity to build on what we have done. That doesn't mean simply running on existing policies in education and in the health service. It means a new start.

What we have done already gives us a position of strength. We can build on that. But we could see the strength slip away in the competitive world if we are not prepared to be innovative and radical.

We will get the responsibility for building enterprise - and the enterprise culture - in Scotland. The Parliament and Executive will be responsible for education and training. They will be responsible for the Enterprise network.

So there is the challenge for the new institutions. Make Scotland a world-beater. Capture the energy which devolution will release. Tap the potential of the Scottish people. Equip Scottish business to compete.

But do not try to do all that by pretending that Scotland alone has all the answers. Learn from the best around the world. Encourage the best to come to Scotland. Welcome the competition which will hone the best in Scottish business.

Without prosperity so much else of what we aspire to achieve for Scotland will be so much more difficult. But the Parliament and the Executive should not see prosperity as an end in itself.

It should be the means to a better and fairer society. We need better education to provide opportunities for those who have missed out.

We want people in work because work gives them the chance to build a better life and in so doing contribute to the community.

The great challenge for Scottish Parliamentarians is to build an inclusive Scotland.

The institutions which can help shape an inclusive Scotland have remained Scottish, and their identities strong. We are proud of our legal system, our history of educational attainment. We have a long tradition of civic involvement and local government. Much of the business of central government has long been administered in Scotland. But the key difference is that from now on Scottish Ministers will be accountable for their policies and decisions to The Scottish Parliament.

We have claimed a community ethic. We have consistently rejected the political expression of a dogma, which asserts the narrow interests of the individual over community values.

The test of a political system is its practical impact on the lives of human beings. We still live in a world where the rewards are ill divided and the concerns of those who fought for progress fifty years ago are still horribly relevant.

It was Tawney who, considering the limits of pond life, argued that intelligent tadpoles

> *"reconcile themselves to the inconveniences of their position by reflecting that, though most of them will live and die as tadpoles and nothing more, the more fortunate of the species will one day shed their tales, distend their mouths and stomachs, hop nimbly onto dry land and croak addresses to their former friends on the virtues by means of which tadpoles of character and capacity can rise to be frogs."*

The consolation that this theory offers for social evils is that exceptional individuals can succeed in evading them.

It is a warning against the common fallacy that holds that if the lad of pairts from a poor background can fight his way to the top there can be nothing wrong with the system.

It is still an uncomfortable metaphor for our society today. What we need is vision and determination. The ability to take the much-vaunted belief in community and make it work. We must have the courage to attack the forces of inertia hiding behind traditional values. That is the challenge. That is what we need radicalism for. That is the true end of politics.

Yes, constitutional change matters. Yes, we must get it right. But I am not standing for The Scottish Parliament to prolong a debate on constitutional change. I don't want to be a frog lecturing tadpoles.

I want a Scotland which will fight social exclusion.

I want an Executive which promotes prosperity and uses that wealth to fight poverty.

I want an Executive which sets high standards for our schools because our children deserve nothing less.

I want a Scottish Executive which shares in the modernisation of the welfare state, working with Westminster to build a better Britain.

And I want that to be our debate - not a wrangle over whether we do or do not tear ourselves out of the Union, but working together to make a stronger Scotland within a stronger United Kingdom.

Modernisation matters now. There is no time to waste. But there are those who would waste it.

We have been trying to reform our school examination system since Howie delivered his report in 1992 and there are still politicians today who will argue for further delay.

There is the challenge of land reform. We are committed to give a legal right for those who live and work the land to bid if that land comes on the market. We are using the New Opportunities Fund to back social progress but there are still many who obstruct and complain.

The need to banish the blight that has affected our housing stock is pressing - the failures of the past are there for all to see. We have set out suggestions for dealing with the debt, providing new ways to manage housing based on community ownership. And yet we meet too often the false charge of privatisation from those apparently ready to live with the errors of the past.

The biggest hospital building programme in NHS history is derided because it uses private partnership cash.

I tell you again the test of a political system is its practical effect on the lives of human beings. The new Edinburgh Royal Infirmary has been discussed for over 30 years - we are going to deliver it. That is what matters.

The challenge is clear. Too many have been excluded.

Big numbers trip lightly off the tongue. Every component digit is a trust betrayed, an opportunity denied, a promise broken.

31,000 unemployed and claiming benefit for over a year. Around a quarter of a million children living in workless households. A quarter of council housing damp. 4,000 youngsters leaving school every year without even one Standard Grade.

Life expectancy in Drumchapel is 7 years less for women and 10 years less for men than in comfortable, next-door Bearsden.

On average in Scotland, 47 per-cent of children leaving school go on to further and higher education. In Springburn, the figure is 4 per-cent. Trust betrayed, opportunity denied.

We can do something about that. We must. We already have.

We have attacked exclusion through the tax and benefit systems. The Working Families Tax Credit will guarantee every family an income of at least £190 a week. No family with earnings of less than £220 a week will pay tax. We are increasing child benefit by £2.95 a week, the largest rise ever. The poorest families will receive a further £2.50 a week for each child under 11.

We will guarantee all pensioners a minimum income of not less than £75 a week and pensioner couples £116 a week.

The National Minimum Wage will help to ensure a decent income for those in work. We will make work worthwhile.

Our agenda for education will not just equip our workforce for the future. It will give decent learning opportunities to all Scotland's children.

Our action on childcare will enable many more parents to take up jobs. But it will particularly benefit lone parents who have not been able to find decent, affordable childcare.

Our investment in health will lead to better and quicker treatment for everyone. But it will focus too on health inequalities, address the disparities in healthcare - and health - between richer and poorer areas.

We need innovative approaches to tackling exclusion. All too often the causes of exclusion are concentrated: on individuals or families, on particular areas.

Too often in the past the assistance to lift people out of exclusion has come in disconnected packages.

The need is for help which is well targeted, effective and straightforward. We need government that delivers.

That is why the New Community Schools programme matters - co-ordinating the delivery of education, health and social services through the school.

The New Deal for Communities will test new ways of making services accessible to local people. Social Inclusion Partnerships will encourage joint working to tackle social exclusion in some of our most deprived communities.

What we are addressing here are long-term problems, with deep roots. Some of what we have already done already shows results; but some will take longer to work into the grain of everyday lives. The Parliament and the Executive must take forward what we have started.

Scottish Ministers working with the Parliament will have direct responsibility for the policies which will shape Scottish solutions to Scottish needs. Education, training, housing, healthcare, economic development: the opportunities to promote an inclusive Scotland will be in their hands.

These powers must be used wisely. The problems we are tackling are real problems, deep-rooted problems. Dealing with these requires - will require - grit, determination and experience. We can build on what we have begun. But we must recognise the scale of the undertaking. We must put it at the centre of Scottish politics for the next decade. We must work for the long term.

Introspection will not solve our problems. Nor will preoccupation with constitutional point-scoring. Responding to the needs of the Scottish people is what matters. Openness to new ideas, to new ways of doing things.

We have started to build a system which will encourage that response, that openness. In the very shaping of the political structure of the Parliament we have designed it to be truly representative. We did not have to introduce proportional representation. It was not obviously in our short-term political interests. But I am convinced it will make a better Parliament, a Parliament working in for the long-term interests of the Scottish people.

We have taken that spirit of openness into decisions on how the Parliament will work. Proposals will come from the Consultative Steering Group, so effectively driven by Henry McLeish. The CSG is cross-party, and includes a range of other interests. Its task is to help establish a framework within which the Parliament will be able to serve the Scottish people and to involve them in its decision making. It will be up to the Parliament to make the final choices. Up to those elected to the Parliament to make it work. I want that challenge. I look forward to it.

The settlement we have created reflects the will of the people of Scotland. We have asserted our democratic right to democratic control in Scotland of policies for Scotland. We have done so not just because it is our democratic right. We have done so because it will give us the chance to build a better Scotland while retaining our links with the rest of the country.

So there is the challenge to The Scottish Parliament and Scottish Ministers.

Build an inclusive society, an outward looking and prosperous society. Found it on fairness and opportunity for all.

Do it by listening to the people of Scotland, by looking outward to learn from the best elsewhere.

That is what the people of Scotland want, that is what they deserve. And I am confident that is what they will get.

The vision is a lifetime of opportunity for all Scottish families. The new Government of Scotland must pledge itself to the making of the new Scotland.

I am proud that the Government in which I serve has taken the lead in constitutional and social reform. We have thrown achievement into the face of cynicism. I am proud of the new electoral system and of the way in which we have encouraged the better representation of women in politics.

But the real task is to include every citizen in the political process. To make an impact upon the economic and social forces which have stunted Scottish lives and destroyed Scottish opportunities.

The next decade must not be one long embittering fight over further constitutional change. For me, the question now is what we do with our Parliament, not what we do to it.

Louis MacNiece in 1938 describing his part in a by-election, wrote:

> *And what am I doing it for?*
> *Mainly for fun, partly for a half-believed-in*
> *Principle, a core*
> *Of fact in a pulp of verbiage,*
> *Remembering that this crude and so-called obsolete*
> *Top-heavy tedious parliamentary system*
> *Is our only ready weapon to defeat*
> *The legions' eagles and the lictors' axes.*

Our job is to improve on that.

Last St Andrew's Day, I was proud of Scotland for delivering the referendum result we needed to secure the devolution settlement.

This St Andrew's Day, I am proud that the Scotland Bill we published a year ago is now an Act.

On St Andrew's Days to come, I want us to be able to look back with pride and forward with confidence.

# SCOTLAND AND EUROPE: BACK IN THE MAINSTREAM

*William and Mary Lecture, The Hague - 8 December 1999*

We are linked by history.

I stand in the hall of this great and ancient university where Scots lawyers studied and shaped the law of our land. I speak under the title of the William and Mary Lecture; a Dutch king who with his Stuart consort acceded to the joint crowns of Scotland and England.

That I have been invited to deliver this lecture tonight is witness to the fact that our paths still run together.

Scotland has embarked on a new era. We have witnessed a rare event: the creation of a new Parliament in a settled democracy.

That is a profoundly important change for Scotland. But it is a change which has been watched with profound interest in Europe and elsewhere in the world.

This lecture is one manifestation of that interest. I witnessed the strength of that interest at first hand in the warm welcome given to the opening of our new office - Scotland House - in Brussels.

This interest I find heartening. I see in it evidence of goodwill towards Scotland and towards the programme of constitutional change on which we are embarked in the United Kingdom.

But it also puts a responsibility on us. As other parts of the world struggle to democracy, as other peoples strive to find a path of prosperous co-existence, our experience in Scotland can stand as an example of peaceful and successful democratic renewal.

That gives me the main theme for my address tonight. The title of this talk is "Scotland and Europe: back in the mainstream" - unusually for me I will stand close to that theme.

Devolution for me is not about Scotland's domestic affairs alone. It is and has been also about Scotland's place in a wider world: in the UK naturally enough, but also in Europe and beyond.

It is my deeply held belief that the changes we have experienced since May 1997 have brought Scotland back into the European mainstream. That says much about Scotland, about the UK and about Europe. That is the territory I want to explore tonight.

We can all be guilty of parochialism, of taking the narrow view. I have found it salutary in speeches I have made over the years to remind my audience of Scotland's European heritage.

Geographically we may be on the north-western periphery of Europe.

But in all dimensions of our life, culturally, socially and economically, our ties to our fellow Europeans are strong. I say that not to prove a point, but to celebrate our European identity.

Sometimes I find the time to indulge my curiosity for our history. Again and again, I am struck by the richness of Scotland's European role. Sometimes we act as though international exchange arrived only with the jet plane. But in many ways we are still re-learning the ease of interchange which came naturally to our predecessors.

I have already mentioned the passage of Scottish lawyers through this university. It intrigues me to learn that one of our fundamental legal texts, the Institutes of the Law of Scotland, was published by the Lord Stair, James Dalrymple, while he was in exile in Leiden from 1682 to 1688. He returned in the ship that took William of Orange to Torbay and the crown of two countries.

Stair's Institute is the great foundation work in Scots law - ordered, rigorous, comprehensive. He picked his way through the political ambushes of Cromwells Commonwealth and the Restoration - a man of principle though it is recorded his prudence did not at all times allow him to make a noise!

Leiden University was home to many Scots - a long tradition of friendship and mutual interest - Gilbert Jack reached Leiden in 1603 teaching philosophy and physics there for upwards of 20 years. He had the good taste to turn down the Chair of Moral Philosophy at Oxford in 1621.

The connection with the law was remarkable - famous names (in Scottish terms at least) like Sir John Clerk of Penicuik who in the 1690s studied under Johanes Voit. Between 1661 and 1750 nearly 40 per-cent of the advocates admitted to the Scottish bar had studied law in the Netherlands. It is an astonishing figure.

I should add in case the connection is seen as too civilised that Scots mercenaries plunged with a will into the religious wars of the 17th century in this country. They were liberally sprinkled through the struggles of the period and one learned monograph calculates - how I know not - that they made up as much as seven per-cent of the Dutch army of the period.

The web runs both ways. Europe was greatly influenced by the thinkers of the Scottish Enlightenment in the 1780s such as Adam Smith, David Hume, Francis Hutcheson and Dugald Stewart. The books of our great romantic novelist, Walter Scott, found their way onto many a European library shelf. In Scotland our monarchs bravely tried to build Renaissance palaces, our east coast merchants and tradesmen copied Dutch vernacular architecture.

There are moments when this richness of interchange is distilled. Not three weeks ago, I was involved in successful moves to secure the retention in Scotland of the great Botticelli painting, "The Virgin Adoring the Sleeping Christ Child".

Some cried foul. Why should we spend good Scottish pounds on Italian art? That is to betray our past. The cultural revolution which Botticelli represents was as important to Scotland as the thought of Adam Smith was and is to economic theory in this century.

Some might wonder whether Scottish ties run these days more to the west than the east. Twenty million Americans, after all, claim Scottish ancestry.

But one does not deny the other.

We can celebrate the richness of culture and endeavour which Scotland sent, and continues to send, into the English-speaking world. But when the offspring of the Scottish Diaspora return, they come back to a place rooted in its European identity.

If I claim that we have brought Scotland back into the European mainstream, I must believe that for a while we were adrift.

In what way?

Whatever the turmoils of the past, our common membership of the European Union has drawn the political currents in the member states closer together. From the clamour of disparate and often discordant political traditions, we have coalesced around a single polity - liberal democracy.

One vitally important strand, apparent across the continent over the last three decades, has been the principle of subsidiarity. It is an ungainly word for an elegant concept. Derived, I believe, from the Catholic social thinkers in Germany in the late 19th century, the practical expression is simple: that public decision-making should take place at the most appropriate level.

You do not manage the emptying of the bins of Leiden from the Hague; you do not attempt to formulate a European defence policy from the town hall.

That strand of political theory found concrete expression across the continent in the 1970s, '80s and into the '90s. Some federal states like Germany had long enshrined constitutionally the division of power and the role of their regions. In other states like France and Spain there was an active process of devolution of power and authority to regional assemblies.

For too long, the United Kingdom stood aside from that trend. By the 1990s, I think it fair to claim that the UK was the most centralised state of the European Union.

We were out of kilter.

We were losing the benefits of the rich developing layer of regional politics in Europe. This was given formal expression in the European Union through the creation of the Committee of the Regions. But it has a far more vivid existence through the dynamism of individual regions and the interchanges between them.

Those who lost most from this increasing divergence of UK from continental experience were the Scots themselves. They voted in election after election for parties committed to the devolution of power to Scotland. For year after year, they saw their own MPs outvoted on Scottish issues and Scottish legislation in the Westminster Parliament.

It is easy to argue that the majority rules. The system did not take account of the distinct religious tradition, different administrative structures, the existence over the 300 years since the Union of the Parliaments of a totally separate body of Scottish domestic statutes passed into law by Westminster.

The reforms introduced by the Labour Government since May 1997 have redressed the balance. We have recognised the legitimate democratic aspirations of the different parts of the UK.

We have done away with the anachronism of hereditary peers voting in the House of Lords. We have established Regional Development Agencies in England. We will have a mayor in London.

We have an Assembly in Wales, a Parliament in Scotland and - perhaps the biggest breakthrough of all - a power-sharing Executive in Northern Ireland.

What does devolution do? Simply put, it restores to democratic control in Scotland those things which are best managed in Scotland. Our Parliament has powers over education and health, transport and economic development, agriculture and the environment, housing and planning.

This is decision-making at the right level. This is about finding Scottish solutions to meet Scottish needs.

We have had our modest controversies on route. The learning curve has been steep. But when we look back with the safety of hindsight, I believe that which will impress most is the speed with which a working Parliament and Executive has been established.

The ground had been well prepared by the Scottish Constitutional Convention representing a wide sweep of Scottish opinion. But when we came to power in May 1997 we had a mountain to climb.

We had to translate the hopes and aspirations of the Constitutional Convention and of the Scottish people into hard edged legislation. We had to design a new Parliament and a new system of government.

We had to manage a Bill through Westminster, negotiating hard with every Department in Whitehall. We had to create a stable settlement around the myriad of issues which are the concern of modern government. We had to shine a light into many dark corners which had lain hidden from view in the complexities of the old regime. We had a Referendum to win, an election to organise and run. We had a Parliament and an Executive to bring into life and full function.

I think that we can claim some modest credit for the success of that process.

We have taken risks certainly when measured against the settled patterns of British politics. We have introduced a proportional voting system reflecting again the mainstream of European politics. It was an example of political masochism or high principle according to taste. My own party abandoned the comfortable first-past-the-post bonus which saw a party taking 40 per-cent of the Scottish vote taking 60 per-cent and more of the seats. The indefensible situation which saw the Conservative party taking near 20 per-cent of the vote and winning not a single seat has gone but with it the stability, the clear and simple power of majority government has been undermined. In the new Scottish Parliament Partnership, coalition administration has come. A new agility is required.

But we are already seeing results.

A programme of eight Bills before The Scottish Parliament where before we were lucky to see two. A Programme for Government, capturing the spirit of our coalition and our common endeavour, setting out the key objectives on which the Executive will deliver in the lifetime of this Parliament. A programme to build social justice, setting out a rigorous plan with milestones and targets towards our objective of eliminating poverty in Scotland.

I said that devolution has been about Scotland's place in the wider world - in the UK as well as in Europe and beyond; about a return to the mainstream in Europe. We have also regained our proper standing within the United Kingdom. In the over-centralised pre-devolution state, all important links had effectively to be with London. Now that has changed - two events this month mark the extent of the change.

First, within the United Kingdom we have now established Joint Ministerial Committees over areas of policy which throw up shared problems. Politicians in devolved administrations and in Central Government will sit down together to seek agreement where they have joint responsibilities for such contrasting areas as poverty and information technology. Co-operation must be the key to success. If poverty is to be checked and rolled back the Scottish Executive must deliver on child care, pre-5 education, an effective health service and decent housing. But this is not enough in itself. Fiscal and Social Security policies are an essential complement.

Devolved government strengthens our democracy but in no way weakens the central need for co-operation and co-ordination. As a result of long wished for progress in Northern Ireland we now have a new institution, the Council of the Isles, which will bring together the leaders of Scotland, Northern Ireland, Wales, the island groups of the United Kingdom and the UK itself for joint discussion and deliberation. These developing links should not be built on narrow political issues but on common interests which I know already exist - the environment, tourism, higher education exchanges and interests relating to business and trade. I am reminded by this that there can also be a return to traditional links with countries, regions, ports, towns outside the United Kingdom. Historically we have been close but over the years we have allowed the traditional connections to lapse.

This is devolution showing its mettle. This is devolution working.

And it will continue to work for Scotland, because it is right for Scotland.

There has been another re-engagement, another way in which we have returned to the European mainstream.

When we came to power in May 1997, the influence of the United Kingdom in the affairs of Europe was at a low ebb. Relations had been soured by the BSE saga.

That was about more than beef. It carried with it a wave of frustration and anger at the indecision of the then Government over its European role. British policy was for a time held to ransom by a faction with a visceral antipathy to Europe.

We wanted to put that right. Tony Blair has talked about ending the ambivalence of the United Kingdom towards Europe. He has worked hard and patiently to rebuild, to re-establish the trust of our partners in our commitment to the common endeavour.

And there has been welcome movement.

We have successfully argued the case to make economic reform a European priority. Together with our partners, we have pioneered a new European employment policy. We used our Presidency to inject new momentum into the Single Market. With key allies, we have managed to cap the growth in EU spending.

In all of this, we have protected legitimate UK interests. Without hysteria and tantrum, we have protected our rebate. We have safeguarded our national border controls. We won a good deal for the UK in the reform of the structural funds. We have hopefully achieved the ending of the beef ban.

Scotland is getting the benefits of this constructive engagement. Our exporters will benefit from a strengthened Single Market. The people of the Highlands and Islands will benefit from the settlement agreed in the negotiations on the structural funds. Scottish beef will lead the way back into European markets.

This is how it should be. This is where our interests lie. The big numbers speak for themselves. Scotland's huge success as a place for inward investment as a base within the European Union. The hundreds of thousands of jobs which depend on the Single Market; the sixty per cent of our exports which leave for destinations in other member states. Predictably our biggest market for manufactured goods and services is the rest of the United Kingdom but Europe as a whole is becoming our arena as the internal market grows and integrates.

The UK is back at the table. Devolution ensures that Scotland plays a full part.

I spoke earlier of the opening of Scotland House in Brussels. That is the visible symbol of our engagement with the European Union. It brings together the Scottish Executive and other Scottish interests in Brussels to provide a coherent focal point for our engagement with matters European.

Scotland House is one part of a web of relationships which ensures the protection of Scottish interests. Appropriately, Scotland House stands over the road from the home of the United Kingdom Permanent Representation in Brussels. We work together with the rest of the UK to advance UK interests and are the stronger for that. The devolution settlement ensures that the voice of the Scottish Executive is heard in the formulation of UK policy, that Scottish Ministers can join the UK delegation to the Council of Ministers.

But there is more to Europe than negotiation and legislation. It would be a poorer place if co-operation stopped at the political level. Beneath the legislative crust, there is a burgeoning of exchange and interaction, often mediated from region to region.

Already we have Finnish and Swedish regions working from Scotland House. We have well developed links to other parts of the EU. Now with our own Parliament, we can make the most of the enthusiasm for the opportunities in Europe.

This is Scotland back in the mainstream. A Scotland benefiting from the devolution of power so long enjoyed in other parts of Europe. This is Scotland in a reinvigorated United Kingdom, re-engaged with Europe.

In this Scotland, we look to three levels of identity: Scottish, British and European.

Many of you here will share those different levels of loyalty, to your locality and region, to your country and to Europe. For me, it is a positive relationship, a dynamic synergy of interest where each enriches the other.

But it is not without challenge.

There is the challenge from the Eurosceptics. To be truly British, I cannot be European. There is the challenge from the nationalist. To be truly Scottish, I cannot be British.

These challenges betray a common mindset.

What is it that links them?

It is the urge to reinstate the boundaries, to strengthen the barriers which divide people from people.

Do not be taken in by the words, the special vocabulary. The Eurosceptic call for "renegotiation" of our membership of the European Union is code for exit from the European Union. The nationalist slogan "Independence in Europe" is close to a contradiction in terms, a nationalist schizophrenia - openness to Union at one level while denying it at another.

What is the Eurosceptic argument? A confused mix of prejudice and fear. They insist that the Earth is flat when we all know that it is round. They ignore the logic of the world in which we live.

Put simply, the European Union has been the anchor of peace and prosperity in Europe for these last 45 years.

Nothing succeeds like success. The countries of east and central Europe and beyond look to become members of the European Union because they know that it will help to guarantee their stability and their economic growth.

The benefits cascade into so many areas where we share a common interest. Into the world of trade where we can together forge a European presence in the globalised market place. Into the world of foreign policy, where the European Union gives us the framework in which we can learn to act together to project a common European voice.

Into the Single Market, where we have built together a market place of 380 million citizens, working to one set of enforceable rules, not complicated by 15 different jurisdictions. Into the sphere of the environment, where common action is trying to tackle the threats of pollution and environmental degradation which respect no boundary.

This is a massive enterprise. The path has not always been smooth or easy. The compromises and political deals which edge the European Union forward can often seem opaque, even threatening, to the citizen. The machinery can appear remote, the decisions arbitrary. We have been poor at explaining the benefits.

There are of course times when all governments have to take into account the reality of national interest. Take the United Kingdom and the Euro. The position of the UK Government is clear. There are no constitutional barriers to membership. But the economic conditions must be right. To join at the wrong moment, when economic cycles are at the wrong point, would do no one any good. To join at the right time will benefit both the UK and Europe.

The European Union has had to learn to move forward while accommodating national interest. I have faith in that continued capacity. It will keep the European Union strong into the next century. It will defeat the warped ideology of the Eurosceptics.

If the Eurosceptics are the Flatearthers, what are the nationalists? Their world is more complex than that of the Eurosceptic. The nationalist roots run deep, back through the centuries. Nationalism has been both the rallying cry for oppressed minorities and the cause of bitter conflict.

Both varieties are still to be seen in Europe today, blurring at the edges in the frightening complexities of the Balkans and in the Caucasus further to the east.

Happily, the nationalism we face in Scotland is of neither ilk. Some nationalist hearts might beat quicker to the Braveheart drum but British and indeed Scottish politics are tolerant. A nation which provides the Chancellor of the Exchequer, the Foreign Secretary, the Secretary of State for Social Security and the Lord Chancellor - and some might even claim the Prime Minister himself - in the UK Government can hardly be said to be dispossessed. Nor is our nationalism a nationalism of bomb and gun.

It is based on a simpler premise: that Scotland would be better off apart from the UK. Simple, but like the Flat Earth Eurosceptics, a defiance of all logic. Where the Flatearthers deny that the Earth is round, the nationalists attempt to defy gravity, the gravity which holds us in the United Kingdom.

Let me explain why.

That separation would benefit Scotland is an untested assertion. All the evidence shows that separation would be economic pain and no gain.

Look at the international level. The reality is that we are part of an international economy and an international polity where we can contribute, punch our weight.

Our trade interests are negotiated in the World Trade Organisation. Our defence is assured through NATO. Our interests in world peace are mediated through the United Nations.

In trade, increasingly in defence and foreign policy, and in so many other spheres, we work together with our partners in the European Union.

What gain for Scotland in peeling away from the UK? Surely no gain in influence in international affairs. Rather a loss of the security we get from working together with the rest of the United Kingdom as one of the European Union's bigger member states, a leading member of NATO, a member of the G7 and of the UN Security Council.

The Nationalists protest their allegiance to a Scotland "independent in Europe". There is and always has been the smack of expediency. Europe was for many in the party endorsed as an insurance against the charge of separatism. The leaders were anxious to rebut the accusation that their party stood for isolation committed as it is to withdrawal from both the UK and NATO. The European vision and the claim of a seat at the top table offered some protection.

In recent times the "independent" Scottish pound has become a more and more troublesome concept. Faced with the prospect of shadowing the English pound loyalty to the Euro provides a useful escape route. Nationalists object to interests rates being set on a uniform basis across the UK but are happy to accept that a common rate should run across Europe. It is an old heresy in a party which has always stressed the right to set an internal rate for Scotland alone as a definitive necessity.

Another powerful force is the energy released by devolution.

Through The Scottish Parliament, we have the power in Scotland to grow our economy. Increasingly, growth potential is released through the dynamism of regional economies. Devolution gives us the chance to access that dynamism. At the moment in Scotland inflation is stable, mortgages and long term interest rates historically low, productivity increasing in both the manufacturing and service sectors, the unemployment claimant count at its lowest level for 23 years. The opportunities are there.

Through The Scottish Parliament, we have the power in Scotland to make the difference; to manage those things best managed in Scotland. We have the power to get our health record right. We have the power to make our educational system a world beater.

Separation would add nothing to our efforts there. Nationalism does not provide a *deus ex machina* to magic away the problems we face. We already know the challenges before us. We have the power - and the responsibility - to face them.

These are essentially negative reasons for opposing separatism. It adds nothing. There is no gain.

But it also takes away. I believe that the union that is the United Kingdom brings incalculable but real benefits to Scotland. With separatism, we would face the pain and the loss of those positive benefits.

England and Scotland have grown to political and democratic maturity together. We have together assured the rule of law, built a welfare state, encouraged our communities.

This is about more than sentiment.

It is about a mutual protection of a common interest. Common action to build and maintain stability. Common action to tackle poverty.

On all these fronts, action is better at the UK level. That is why economic policy, taxation and benefit awards which run evenly across the land are reserved to the UK Government. Because we are better off working as a team.

You don't share the same house for nigh on 300 years without gaining a certain familiarity, a certain intimacy. There is a line on a map which marks the border between England and Scotland. But it is a line which Scots and English cross freely, without let or hindrance, to live, to work, to do business, to study, to play and to marry.

Why unlearn what so many in the world are desperately seeking to learn, the will to live as one with our neighbour?

Two challenges, the Eurosceptic and the nationalist. Two challenges which resonate to different degrees in different parts of Europe.

I do not underestimate their residual strength. But I am optimistic that their challenge will be seen off.

Why?

Because I see Eurosceptic and nationalist, both, stranded by the shifting course of history, both defying logic, both defying the best interests of Scotland, both shouting their ineffectual slogans from the sandbanks.

I claimed earlier three identities. I am Scottish, I am British, I am European. I will carry those identities into the new year and into the new century, confident that they will endure. Endure because each, individually and together, lends us the strength we need to prosper in this world in which we live.

# IRISH-SCOTTISH ACADEMIC INITIATIVE CONFERENCE

*Dublin - 29 September 2000*

Political dialogue is not always easy in my country. There are, of course, persistent practitioners. I met a gentleman the other day who almost literally attached himself to me under the incurable delusion that I was Robin Cook. He conducted a one-sided discussion on the need for an ethical foreign policy through five blocks.

Recently I was accused of being an animadverter - someone who talks reasonably fluently, looking at a subject from every side but coming to no very obvious conclusions. It is an art form and one I have been practising for many years without necessarily achieving competence. I have no intention of changing my habits tonight.

I am very conscious of the fact that I am not an expert on Irish or indeed Scottish history and inevitably tend to parade my particular political prejudices. I may do a little of that on the margins this evening. I mention this as a health warning. I am very conscious that there are a very large number of people in this audience very much better qualified than I am to lead discussion on the topics of the night.

One of the by-products of recent developments in Scotland, and indeed the United Kingdom as a whole, is a broader more understanding concern and an appreciation of the Irish connection. In the past the Irish and their descendants in Scotland have been under-valued, under-researched and too often forgotten. It is partly political - I have a constituency in the west of Glasgow strongly influenced by Irish immigration. I have often been struck by the wish to avoid discussion about the troubles in Northern Ireland or my views on the options being canvassed at the time. The great thing is that tolerance has grown and the tensions which at one time were very evident in West Central Scotland have now very largely faded.

I ought to note at this point that there are skilled commentators who would regard such a view as complacent. But I believe that in terms of the economy and the distribution of jobs prejudice is now almost unknown. Shadows, of course, can linger, but prejudice if discovered is derided. I remember well a by-election in industrial Lanarkshire. There was an ecumenical meeting organised by all the churches. The first question came from a gentleman, apparently a pillar of respectability, whose question to the SNP candidate was that he understood that in an independent Scotland there would be nothing to stop the Prime Minister being a Catholic and what was she prepared to do to combat this very obvious danger. To the spectators it seemed like a voice from another age, from another time.

Scotland is a welding of many traditions and peoples. It is not a homogeneous nation. It grew. It evolved. We have over the centuries benefited enormously from the ideas, the inspiration, the cultural patterns of those who have moved into our land.

Ireland and the Irish have been great forces affecting Scottish history and attitudes in very different ways. First and most obviously there is the Gaelic tradition which has had and still has so great an influence - a culture which once covered much of Scotland. Boundaries were vague concepts in medieval times. We know so little about the lives of ordinary people all those years ago. I remember a learned correspondence in the Herald newspaper about Robert the Bruce and in particular what language he spoke on his family lands in Carrick. After much coming and going, there was a general assumption that it would be some form of Gaelic but clearly no one really knew.

Today there are only 50-60,000 Gaelic speakers in Scotland but the Gaeltacht is still of enormous importance. It is an entity which stretches from the Butt of Lewis to the Dingle Peninsula in the South of Ireland. I was delighted to hear last Friday in Stornoway that the Western Isles Council has formalised links with both County Clare and the District of Newry and Mourne in Northern Ireland. These developments can only be good news.

There has been publicity recently for a study by David Crystal which suggests that a great many of the world languages are literally disappearing and that a threshold of perhaps 100,000 or certainly above 60,000 speakers is necessary for survival. It is dangerous to work with simple extrapolations. Where a community is determined to keep its language it can and will do so. Gaelic has survived neglect, indeed suppression, perhaps even oppression over many years. Today there is a widespread public sympathy and understanding and the commitment of the Gaelic speaking community are more powerful than any set of statistical projections.

We have made great strides with Gaelic medium education, Gaelic broadcasting and now with encouraging education in Gaelic symbolised perhaps by the Sabhal Mor Ostaig which stands so handsomely just outside Armadale on the Sleat peninsula and which will be an integral and increasingly important part of the University of the Highlands and Islands as it develops.

I was there recently. There was a great ceilidh in the evening and a shinty/hurling match in the afternoon though I fear it might fall rather far short of the atmosphere of 80,000 in Croke Park.

There is no doubt that the legacy of Gaelic culture has permeated the whole of Scotland. The written word may be a mystery but Gaelic song has become one of the hallmarks of cultural revival. Someone like myself who has not got the language can still appreciate and connect with all sorts of Gaelic cultural expressions. I defy any Scot to hear a Gaelic psalm led by a Presaenter wherever he may be in the world and not know exactly what he was hearing.

But Irish influence is not simply part of the great traditions, important though they are stretching back to Iona to the Book of Kells, the storytellers and the Lordship of the Isles. Ireland has also had a major influence on Scotland in much later times and in a wider context.

For long enough, indeed arguably from Harlaw to Culloden, the Highlands with its Irish influence was seen as a dangerous savage land by lowland Scots. Indeed there are examples of the Highlands making common cause even with England in the stand against the efforts of the medieval Scottish Kingship to extend its influence.

But when Scotland was reinvented in the early 19th century by Walter Scott, by Lady Nairne, by the new romanticism - the rehabilitation of the Highlands was well under way. Pitt the Younger discovered the virtue of the Highland soldier proven in the North American wars on the Heights of Abraham. Soon romanticism had produced a vision of Highland culture. Victorians had begun to admire the wilderness and the Queen herself had built Balmoral.

In the intervening years however there had been much trouble. The population of the Highlands grew right through to the 1820s till checked by the collapse of the kelp industry the arrival of the cheviot and the black face and the great economic famine of 1847 which provided a traumatic backdrop to the clearances. We shared with Ireland, the potato blight and some of all that that meant. It was a terrible time though it is worth remembering that the Highland Chieftain was in many ways as culpable as the great noblemen living opulently in London. After all there were plenty like MacLean of Coll who cleared Rum sending almost the entire population to Canada in 1826. The island ultimately passed to the Marquis of Salisbury who introduced deer.

One of the great links with Ireland is the land question and the conscience of Mr Gladstone.

He showed a remarkable grasp in 1885 of the issues lamenting that in Scotland the Highland Chieftain had "gradually found that the rearing of men paid him in a coin no longer current and took to the rearing of rent instead". There is a splendid exchange between the Grand Old Man and Sir William Harcourt, the then Home Secretary, recorded in Gladstone diaries. Apparently Mr Gladstone was reading John Stuart Blackie on the 'Scottish Highlands and the Land Law'. Blackie, as some of you may know, was a polymath whose range stretched from lectures on Plato to the war songs of the Germans. Gladstone rather dryly recorded in his diary "I am reading Blackie and the crofters thus far wholly without advantage". A few days later Harcourt replied to the effect that "Blackie is a commentator who too little learning has made mad". We all know one or two like that.

Irish influence certainly contributed to the Land League of the early 1880s led by such men as John Murdoch. It is perhaps interesting to note that Murdoch visited the school at Braes in Skye in early 1882 - around the time of the Battle of the Braes a great incident in Highland history, although perhaps small of scale when compared with experiences in Ireland. His visit to the school was long remembered. One of the children years later recorded that he was "the first man I ever saw wearing a kilt". The teacher refused to allow Murdoch to address the children in Gaelic insisting they speak English. Despite the romanticism, the language and the culture it represented was still under very real pressure.

The Highlands are now in a very special sense a success story. The population of Scotland in 1970 was almost exactly the same as it is today. The increase in the Highland population is 20 per-cent. It is not all oil and Inverness. Last year was a record for inward investment in the region. It is particularly encouraging to see the Highlands benefiting from new technology - lithium batteries in Thurso, call centres in Dingwall and Kinlochleven, the creation of jobs in Stornoway. Information Technology is helping the Highlands overcome the challenge of distance from markets and offering opportunities across the country. It is a trail that I know has been very effectively pioneered here in Ireland.

There are other links, connections, influences. There was the very determined migration of Scots from Ayrshire and the South West into Ireland in the 18th century. I was surprised on a recent visit to Dublin to hear it suggested - by your President no less - that there was a surviving language based on those events.

More important inevitably was the Irish influx after the great famine. A year or two ago I was at a ceremony to mark the 500th anniversary of the Roman Catholic Diocese of Glasgow. It has as an enormously long and honourable tradition built over the years but there is an interesting period of quietude. Around the early years of the 19th century there was no resident Catholic priest in the City of Glasgow. There was neither need nor demand. It is a remarkable thought given the way the face of the City changed. An astonishingly large number of my constituents claim at least a grandparent from Donegal. The Irish community is now established, growing in prosperity. Its mark can be measured by the names of those who write well in Scotland today, Willie McIlvanneys, Andrew O'Hagans and many more.

There is a great debate about the future of the United Kingdom and how it is affected by devolution. The founding text is Linda Colley's analysis of forces that welded together the mosaic that became Great Britain.

From Scotland's point of view and more importantly from England's, there were indeed powerful reasons for union. One was the need to secure the Protestant Succession; another was to shut the back door against the French. These may sound very strange considerations but 1709, 1715 and 1745 were to be reminders of the troubled times against which the Union was meant to guard. The Succession Act was snubbed by The Scottish Parliament with no guarantee that they would follow England in passing over a major scatter of Catholic successors, to instal that least romantic of figures, George Elector of Hanover.

For the Scots there was compensation for the Darien Disaster - that unfortunate ill-starred, ill-equipped attempt to open up a Scottish colony in the wrong place at the wrong time. Entrance to the English colonial markets did ultimately bring prosperity. It was a connection that had the odd ironic twist. Lord Bute was the first Scottish Prime Minister in Britain. He had also the distinction of losing the American colonies.

Henry Dundas, Harry IX, ran the East India company as an outward bound adventure for Scots. Tobacco made Glasgow rich. All forms of trade flourished.

Linda Colley records with remarkable skill the political, but equally importantly the cultural reasons for union. She argues that most of these are now irrelevant and have gone. It is back to Britain having lost an empire and found no role. The implication is that the future is uncertain and that in the age of the European Union and devolved government within the United Kingdom where will the movement end?

Scotland has always maintained a remarkable sense of identity within the Union. This is largely due to the terms hammered out in 1707 which ensured the survival of the Kirk, the primacy of the legal establishment, the future of the Universities - preserving their very separate and ancient traditions. It was a structure that survived and was reinforced over the years by the great if ill-distributed wealth generated by Victorian entrepreneurial skill.

There was a growing cultural confidence but the key fact is that this did not lead to or rely on political expression. Cultural pride is particularly important in both Scotland's present and past.

You can take much time arguing about the nature of the nation state. This morning on the radio learned men were suggesting that Denmark was the most "nationalist" country in Europe. That is building heavily on a snapshot vote which I freely confess disappointed me and many colleagues.

I take the academically simplistic view that nationhood is not necessarily built on race and can only be defined in terms of a coming together of peoples who wish to be regarded as a separate political entity. Language, economic expediency or necessity, the existence of a long tradition may be governing factors. All of this may be underpinned by cultural identity but that identity does not necessarily take a nationalist form.

Scotland is not parochial. Of course as in every community there are those for whom the next street is a foreign country. They are not typical.

Scotland is a small place on the edge of the European continent. It has never been a credible strategy for the Scots to turn inwards, to ignore the wider world. That was never going to be the route to prosperity, to a vigorous cultural life, to a vigorous society.

Take the economy. Scotland is a trading nation. That has been the case for long enough. What brought the Dutch influence to the towns of the East Neuk of Fife? Trade. What supplied the cotton mills of Lanarkshire and absorbed their product? Trade. What were the ships on the Clyde built for? Not to sail up the canal to Edinburgh, but for trade.

We have not lost this trading outlook. In manufactured goods alone, Scottish experts exceeded £20 billion last year. And this excludes the exports to our largest single market - the rest of the UK.

This international perspective is reflected in other ways. Scotland has been a favoured destination for inward investment for many years.

Inward investors come because of the supply of skilled labour, the scientific and engineering base, the quality of life, access to UK and European markets, because Scotland is a good place to do business.

Inward investors have brought jobs and prosperity to Scotland. The Scottish economy has absorbed the benefits of this international exposure, the technological developments, the introduction of new products and processes, the alternative management practices.

Scotland is an open economy. We are open to new ideas and best practice from across the globe. We play our part in the global economy.

What about cultural identity? Two vignettes. Look back to the Scottish Enlightenment of the late 18th Century. The coming together of talents can be seen on the walls of Edinburgh University's courtroom. Clearly the University Authorities wanted an equivalent of a team photograph. They sent for the local man to paint portraits of the luminaries of the day.

The result is magnificent: in a room by Robert Adam hung with portraits by Sir Henry Raeburn - William Robertson, the historian: Adam Ferguson, the philosopher, who pioneered sociology (some would argue it was a great mistake); Playfair and Carstares. To these can be added Hume, Scott and Adam Smith.

Look today to the Edinburgh Festival and Fringe. Together they are a tremendous Scottish success story. Both draw much of their strength from Scottish support and their vitality from Scottish performers and the Scottish cultural repertoire. But both reach out to an international culture and international audiences - and both succeed.

I recommend Lord Cockburn's Memorials as one of the great diaries of the 19th century. A classic work and the man largely with Jeffrey responsible for the 1832 Scottish version of the Reform Act constantly mourned what he saw as the death of all things Scottish. He splendidly condemned all this talk of Bannockburn 'and such nonsense' as doing great harm to the cause of Scotland - the virtues of a distinct culture. Scotland was building North British railways, North British engineering companies, North British hotels.

But there was a subtle change. Scottishness became more and more pervasive. It found an echo even among the highest in the land.

In 1884 the Scottish Office was founded, brought in by the Tories in the unlikely human form of the Duke of Richmond and Gordon.

My favourite example is Henry Campbell Bannerman who in 1885 changed his notepaper. He lived in a fake French chateau in the Perthshire village of Meigle - if you look at his notepaper Belmont Castle moved from NB to Scotland in 1885.

I welcome the growth, welcome the renewed interest. I am excited by the way in which English courses and history courses now accept and require knowledge of our country. I believe it may even be possible to persuade the press to move beyond the constitutional question and to recognise that politics can encompass policy

What has to be decided is whether this is the politics of identity rampant and unstoppable, or whether we can co-exist within a United Kingdom and take a more relaxed view looking out to a wider Europe.

Scottish home rule has long been an ambition of the Left in Scotland. Heavily influenced by Irish nationalism, efforts were made to bring in Home Rule Bills in plenty in the Twenties.

Political Nationalism of course has grown. The SNP from its eccentric roots in the late 1920s had a slow and largely unnoticed start. In 1951 the Party fought only two seats in the General Election and yet by 1974, a mere 20 years later, it won 11 and got 30 per-cent of the popular vote. It is important however to remember that in the year 2000 the party is still finding 30 per-cent a difficult barrier to cross.

The SNP have of course the seeming advantage of having all Scotland to draw on. They are not linguistically based as is the case with the Welsh as the Catalans or indeed nationalists in Quebec.

It is often difficult to read the political runes in Scotland. The big break through for the SNP came in the north-east round Aberdeen. At one time in my career I represented South Aberdeen and I was surrounded by solid Tory seats represented by such worthies as Jock Bruce Garndine, Bob Boothby who had just retired to the Lords and Patrick Walridge-Gordon - Tory majorities that looked immovable. Those voters were the most unlikely nationalists, voting as they had over the years with uncomplaining zeal for the Conservative and Unionist Party. Now they vote nationalist. The question is what do they believe?

Is it no more than the south-north divide which made Whitehall and Westminster unpopular on the Tyne as certainly as on the Clyde? Is the collapse of heavy industry blamed on Governments although part of change that has affected every Western nation? Is it because globalisation has in fact encouraged people to put a new emphasis on their roots, upon a sense of identification with the area from which they come. Is it the disintegration of class hiding an ideological void into which nationalism has grown?

I do not believe that the future lies with the politics of identity - certainly in Scottish terms. There is and should be a welcome for the loosening of the bonds, the more relaxed view of local decision making which now marks Westminster. I do not believe that devolution is a stepping stone, a process which leads inevitably to independence. Nothing is inevitable in politics. I believe the success that is devolution is an end in and of itself - and that Scotland will hold to that.

We have had some alarms and excursions at Holyrood but substantial solid success. Carving a legislative competence out of a unitary state is no easy matter. This year we have passed 12 Executive Bills covering a wide range of issues too long neglected. At Westminster even with sharp elbows in the legislative queue we would be lucky to get two significant Scottish Bills in a session.

The outstanding characteristic is stability. Opponents of devolution now vie to declare their loyalty and their intention to make it work in future. No one wants to go back to what was.

Nationalists may on occasion gather strength on the basis of a protest vote. They are the available option for the discontented. Clearly my own Party has taken a knock in the polls over recent weeks. That does not mean that there is a genuine increase in support for independence. Indeed the most recent poll which brought for me a certain lack of cheer had devolution at 55 per-cent support and independence at 24 per-cent - crumbling and falling from previous highs.

No one can be absolute on these matters. There are fascinating questions about the significance for example of the different performance of the Nationalists in polls recording Westminster as distinct from future Holyrood choices. The SNP promises are always higher when asked about Scottish Parliament elections perhaps because they are seen as exclusively a Scottish option irrelevant at Westminster level.

Mr Hague has been making some fairly warlike noises about changes that he might want to introduce to meet the challenges of change. He should remember that devolution was introduced by Westminster and could not have been implemented without the solid support of my Cabinet colleagues. Mr Hague suggests two classes of MPs with Scottish representatives excluded from voting on what he would define as matters of exclusive English interest. This is a solution examined and rejected by Gladstone all these years ago. It would create different classes of MP in an unacceptable way. I do not believe it would work. If those seeking change see the West Lothian question as a problem what validity is there for them in a proposal that might leave a UK government without a working majority for its 'English' in inverted commas programme.

Scotland is not a place turned in on itself. You see it in the assimilation in Scotland of migrants - Irish, Jews, Poles, Italians, Asians - not, to be sure, without some tensions, but certainly without the bitterness which has too often marred the intermingling of other peoples.

Devolution does not mean a parochial Scotland. It does not mean a return to the kailyard. Inwardness is not the Scottish experience of the past. It is not the Scotland that I know. It will not be the future.

Scotland has always had this international perspective. But the great periods: the Enlightenment of the late 18th Century, the great entrepreneurial explosion of late victorian times, the cultural renaissance of the twentieth century, so important to Scotland's sense of identity, have all occurred within and benefited from and enriched the United Kingdom. They are arguments not for separation but part of the case for a strong Scotland within a strong United Kingdom. And to recognise that is not to belittle or undermine what is Scottish.

Devolution does not, will not, separate Scotland from the rest of the United Kingdom. There is a common heritage, economic links, shared experiences, challenges and opportunities. I believe that we are stronger together, weaker apart.

I keep meeting journalists who tell me that there is a deep anger in Westminster about all matters Scottish. I find it rather odd that the front runner in the election for Speaker is a Scot and that does not appear to be a factor which has in any way adversely influenced his prospects. In devolution, we have a settlement which builds on the strengths of the UK. It puts what is best managed in Scotland to be managed in Scotland. It leaves what is best done at the UK level at the UK level. It recognises our community of interest. It recognises our rights and responsibilities within that community. By getting the balance right, we strengthen our shared commitment to the UK, we reinforce the union.

Devolution is a tribute to the maturity and flexibility of the Union and its ability to adapt to meet the needs of its constituent parts. The whole country, all of us, can take credit for that. Devolution will work, not because of clever drafting or the political equivalent of fancy footwork, but because there will be the good will to make it work. The good will is there because we have a shared outlook on the world. And the roots of that run deep.

When I was a young politician I was influenced by John P MacIntosh, the brilliant if idiosyncratic member for East Lothian. Intellectually he made an enormous contribution to the devolution debate - one of his particular enthusiasms was dual nationality. I reject those who take Linda Colley's arguments about the relevance of the 18th century justification for union to mean that there are no bonds in the 21st century. In a Britain where people inter-marry and inter-mingle both socially and economically, this is evident nonsense.

I am asked what I am. I am a Scot, a citizen of the United Kingdom and someone who has a very real interest in the future of the European Union. I suspect that those priorities and preferences still govern the thinking of the majority of Scots and will continue to dictate the outcome of the continuing argument about constitutional arrangements within Britain.

# Respect Across the Party Divide
## *Political Tributes*

From his University days, where his group of friends included Jimmy Gordon, Menzies Campbell and the late John Smith, through his long years as an MP and latterly as an MSP and First Minister, Donald Dewar worked closely with politicians of all political parties.

His ability to fight Labour's corner in the cut-and-thrust of political debate, yet recognise the undoubted merits of consensual politics gained Donald Dewar friends and respect across all the parties.

Four politicians from the main Parties who served alongside Donald Dewar offer here their tributes.

# The Rt.hon TONY BLAIR MP
*Prime Minister*

The sudden death of Donald Dewar has left a deep sense of loss. He was, indeed, the father of his nation and a huge figure in UK politics. A fond father to his children, Ian and Marion. A trusted colleague and, for me and many others, an extraordinary friend.

Scotland has lost its leader and its guiding hand. It has lost a great man, too. I can imagine how Donald - whose modesty was legendary - would react to these words and all the other tributes but they are nevertheless true.

His qualities of honesty, integrity, wisdom and, perhaps most of all, decency made him a successful and loved politician and an honour to know.

He was not born into a Labour family but very early on, his values of compassion and social justice led him to the Labour Party. He stuck with it through thick and thin and never wavered in his belief that Labour was the political force which would create a stronger, fairer and more just society.

Donald was a fighter. He lost his Aberdeen South seat in 1970 but came back through the tough Garscadden by-election which stemmed the nationalist tide in 1978. He continued to represent the constituency with pride.

For someone of Donald's talents, it was tragic that he should spend so much of his parliamentary career in opposition. But he used his time well. It was Donald, with his lifelong friend John Smith, who built the case for a Scottish Parliament during Labour's years outside government. Like John, he also became a master of the House of Commons. Few commanded the chamber like him.

After the General Election three years ago, it was Donald who drove through the devolution programme. He shaped the White Paper, fought through the Scotland Act and led the referendum campaign from the front.

But history will not just show that Donald Dewar delivered The Scottish Parliament. It will also show that, through his personality, wisdom and leadership, he laid the foundations which will make it a success for the people of Scotland.

His desire for a Scottish Parliament was not borne out of devotion to the niceties of constitutional theory but because he believed it to be a power for good for Scotland and would forge a new and better relationship with the rest of the UK.

He was the only man to be First Minister. It felt right and it was right. The opening day of The Scottish Parliament was, he said, the greatest day of his life. His brilliant speech that day did the historic occasion justice.

To this taxing job of First Minister, he brought his own special blend of political and personal skills. I had more reason that most to know, and be grateful, for his qualities.

He was a valued colleague and a special friend, warm and loyal, whose advice was unfailingly wise and was sweetened by his irreverent and self-deprecating humour. None of us were exempt from his wit, and we loved him for it.

Some were surprised when he became Labour chief whip at Westminster. But he was an outstanding success, winning the respect of MPs from all parts of the Labour party and all parties in the House. In that post, he also played a key role in Labour's election victory and brought his outstanding campaigning skills to an audience throughout the UK.

Donald, of course, was in some ways an old-fashioned politician. He had no time for the modern obsession with personality or appearance. He genuinely didn't care how he looked and couldn't understand why anyone else did. He had to be dragged out complaining by his devoted staff to buy a new coat, shoes or suits.

He numbered many journalists among his friends but for the media in general, his view was that they would have to take him as they found him. And whatever the political problems of the day, for that, he won people's affection and respect.

I was with Donald in Scotland, for what has proved the final time, just a few weeks ago. He seemed to be recovering well from his heart operation although, as ever, it was difficult to prise out such personal information from him.

Among the engagements we shared in a busy day was a business lunch in Glasgow. As we left, we went over together to talk to a sizeable crowd which had gathered outside. What left its mark on me - as it always did when I visited Scotland in his company - was the genuine warmth of his reception and his surprise and embarrassment that so many people wanted to shake his hand.

It was typical of the bond between him and the people of Scotland. Even when times were difficult, they recognised that Donald was always fighting for them.

In an age where the public are cynical about politics, Donald stood out. It was, in some ways, his modesty and down-to earth nature which marked him out as a politician of such stature.

He transcended party politics, winning the respect and affection of those of all political persuasion and none. Among his closest friends were some of the most senior politicians of other parties who will feel his loss as deeply as his many friends in the Labour Party.

Donald was a good friend. A fine politician. A tremendous servant of our party and our country. His passing will leave a vacuum in our national life and the lives of many people which will be difficult to fill. He was, indeed, a thoroughly decent man.

# ALEX SALMOND MSP
*Scottish National Party*

In some fifteen years of political sparring with Donald Dewar in television studios, the Westminster Parliament and more recently the Scots Parliament I suspect I knew him well enough to judge how he would have felt about some of the frothier coverage following his tragic death.

People who knew Donald far better than I have pointed out that he would have regarded the 'Father of the Nation' description with some disdain and perhaps with a wry observation that a nation with a thousand years or so of continuous history is unlikely to have such recent parentage.

For Donald Dewar was an exceptionally well read man and his interests extended well beyond what passes these days for political theory into a deep appreciation and understanding of Scottish history and culture.

I took issue with a number of his views. His concept of Scotland seemed to follow a patrician, almost Whig-like debunking of the romantic, celtic strands of Scottishness. For example, his dismissive opinion of tartan wouldn't fit easily with young Scots who cheerfully use tartan as much as an identity statement as a fashion accessory.

However, without question Donald was a Scottish patriot and I like to think it was this desire to do the right thing by Scotland, which persuaded him to embrace the joint campaign with the SNP in the referendum of August 1997.

A number of his close friends and certainly Downing Street were against this decision believing that it would concede to much ground to the independence position. I found that in the crucial days of mid Summer 1997 that once Donald determined on a united campaign he stuck determinedly to the path he had chosen.

He was well aware that the decision created party difficulties for me just as it created internal problems for him. We therefore worked out a position we could adhere to throughout the campaign and one which was based on principle as well as convenience. We both argued that what brought the devolutionist and independence positions into a joint campaign was our overriding belief in the right of the Scottish nation to determine our own constitutional future whatever it may be.

That position held firmly throughout the campaign and the resounding endorsement that it helped deliver saw off both the token parliamentary resistance from the Tory 'last ditchers' in Westminster, and the potentially more potent blocking and tackling from Donald's own cabinet colleagues.

I like to think that it was this 'spirit of 97' that Donald was again reflecting when he made what was undoubtedly the finest speech of his life at the official opening of Parliament.

"This is about more than our politics and our laws. This is about who we are, how we carry ourselves. There is a new voice in the land, the voice of a democratic Parliament. A voice to shape Scotland as surely as the echoes from our past."

Such a sentiment does not make him the 'Father of the Nation' but the 'Father of the Parliament' - no mean epitaph for any politician.

# LORD JAMES DOUGLAS-HAMILTON MSP
*Scottish Conservative and Unionist Party*

Donald Dewar was one of the most remarkable politicians of his generation. He was a superb debater and as a student his debating prowess became well known when he won the Observer Mace Debating Competition and became President of the Glasgow University Union.

I first met Donald in 1963. We had both been selected for a student conference in West Berlin and I stood one foot away from him in the Central Square of Berlin just in front of the rostrum when President John Kennedy made his famous speech "I am proud to be a Berliner" - a moment of history when the Russian Regime were being informed that they could not invade West Berlin without unacceptable consequences.

We had the extraordinary experience of being guarded by East Berlin border guards, including one with a machine gun when our group attempted unsuccessfully to take gifts to East Berlin families. Even at that stage it was clear that he would have a significant political future and it was no coincidence that he was asked to chair the last session of our conference.

Donald Dewar was extremely good company, knew an immense amount about Nineteenth Century history, and the only time I ever saw him really angry was when a student had mentioned what Donald interpreted to be the possibility of Bishops in the Kirk.

He was soon elected to Parliament for South Aberdeen defeating a woman MP who although I did not know it at the time would become my future mother-in-law, but his stay in South Aberdeen would only be for one Parliament.

Subsequently he would have been selected for Motherwell but he had applied for another seat and felt he could not put in his name. It was typical of his sense of honour. He was re-elected to the House of Commons in a famous by-election for Garscadden at a time of potential SNP upsurge and once again appeared in the House of Commons. As I had been elected shortly before I invited him to lunch if he did not mind being seen with a Tory.

He came and mentioned that he should be voting on a three-line Whip but he had given a promise to Nicholas Fairbairn that he would pair when he was away and therefore having given his word he would incur official displeasure rather than break his promise. This was clear evidence that his word was his bond.

During the years that Labour was in opposition he was an extremely close friend of John Smith. Politically they were both in the mould of Hugh Gaitskell and were centre of the road politicians. They both contributed a considerable service to their party in making Labour more electable, and one of the most moving speeches Donald ever gave was at the service for the late John Smith.

In 1987 Labour had won 50 seats in Scotland and the Tories were reduced to ten seats. I was asked to become a Junior Minister and found it disquieting in the first few hours to be expected to know everything, before having had the opportunity to obtain a complete grasp of a large and new portfolio of responsibilities. At the same time Donald was leader of 50 Scots Labour MPs but not in a position to deliver immediately for them what they wanted, namely a Scottish Parliament.

At that time, I met him by chance outside the Westminster Underground and I think he sensed what was in my mind and he said "I too have problems you know!". His sense of humour and wit would never desert him and on the floor of the House of Commons and in debates in Committee he was extremely formidable.

One traumatic night I shared with him. It was the tragedy of Lockerbie. We arrived at the scene a few hours after the outrage. All that could be seen were small groups of police officers, fire-fighters and soldiers and our eyes were spared the worst of the nightmare as we were anaesthetised by the darkness. The most poignant memory was rows of empty ambulances unable to assist.

Donald was very silent and his only comment was "I never wish to see another night like this as long as I live". There was nothing we could do, but by our presence we were in our own way paying our respects to the dead.

His most important contribution was to pilot the Scotland Bill successfully to the Statute Book, thereby creating the first Scottish Parliament for 300 years. Indeed the greatest speech of his life, in my view, was at the Opening Ceremony of The Scottish Parliament.

He was a very approachable person, and never pretended to be anything other than himself. He was liked and respected and his loss will be keenly felt throughout Scotland.

He had the good fortune to be The Scottish Parliament's First Minister and as David McLetchie has said "his breadth of knowledge, wit and abundant experience as a Parliamentarian will be remembered with warmth and affection by friends and opponents alike. He will have his place in history, not only as the standard bearer for his Party in its most difficult time, but as the man who lived to see the fulfilment of his dream."

# The Rt.Hon MENZIES CAMPBELL MP
*Liberal Democrat*

Hundreds of thousands of words have been written about Donald Dewar since his death.

If I listen carefully, I can hear him dismissing them all as froth with a mixture of irritation and embarrassment in his voice.

I can also hear him being particularly waspish about his instant canonisation by some newspapers and journalists who had made life hell in the last 18 months.

Having, like a good midwife, delivered Home Rule for Scotland, Donald Dewar was then landed with the difficult job of bringing up the infant as well.

It was anything but easy.

Coalition Government was a novelty, but inevitable, and both Labour and the Liberal Democrats failed to understand the need to ensure enough MPs experienced at Westminster offered themselves for the Edinburgh Parliament.

Dewar's dominance at Holyrood was due to many factors. He was older and cleverer than most. He believed passionately in Home Rule. It was the "unfinished business" of his great friend John Smith and he was determined to finish it.

He piloted the legislation through the House of Commons and led the successful campaign to win the referendum which followed.

Donald Dewar was the human face of Home Rule, revered when it went well, first in the firing line when it didn't.

His record in public life was exemplary, his loyalty to his party unchallengeable. In fact, loyalty was one of his most obvious qualities. He was intensely loyal to his friends and he inspired it in them in return. He could be impatient, irascible, awkward and witty, charming and erudite.

He knew more about Scotland's history, literature, poetry and art than anyone else I know. Set him down among another group of friends and his crackling wit would have the whole place in stitches. He was famously christened the "Gannet" at Glasgow University, both for his appetite and his gangling appearance.

And it was at Glasgow University that he found the opportunity in student debating to develop the skills in company with John Smith, which made him such a formidable performer in national politics.

At University, Donald did just enough to get through. Work was a necessary evil, debating and politics were the real interest.

He was proud of Scotland and had the Scottish distaste for airs and graces. He had no time for the style consultants who tried to change his suits and ties so that they were more suitable for the modern television age.

Walking about with Donald Dewar was like a Royal progress. People constantly came up to him to shake his hand, particularly after the massive heart operation from which we all hoped he had made a full recovery. He was touched and genuinely surprised by their affection.

As Jim Wallace said with such feeling and accuracy, Donald Dewar was a loyal, honest and decent man. These qualities made him attractive to politicians and public alike.

There is talk of memorials, of trust funds, of libraries and much else by which to remember him. But his lasting legacy to his beloved country was the Parliament he fought for for most of his political life.

Donald Dewar was not a haughty man but he was a proud one. He had much to be proud about. We can truly say of him: "When will we see your like again?"

# REFLECTIONS OF THE MEDIA

I n the hours and days after Donald Dewar's death, the written and broadcast media were packed with tributes to the late First Minister. Contributions came from political colleagues, friends and the media themselves.

This small selection of tributes features the words of journalists and columnists who knew Donald Dewar well at a personal level, and others whose experiences were of a more reflective nature.

# BRIAN TAYLOR
*BBC's Scottish Political Editor*

It was July the first last year. Scotland's Parliament had been royally opened. The evening celebrations in Edinburgh were long, loud - and authentic. Down the Mound came the procession: French acrobats, samba-style music, huge crowds.

As I mingled with those crowds - duty, you understand, duty - I witnessed politicians dispensing with their customary reserve: or, depending upon your standpoint, behaving according to type. I was hailed joyously by a very senior former civil servant who was leaping like a young thing.

And I witnessed - I swear I did - a remarkable thing. I saw Donald Dewar's shoulder (the left, I think) twitch fractionally in time with the raucously ebullient rhythm as he progressed towards Princes Street. For D. Dewar, this was tantamount to ecstatic release. Donald was, that evening at least, an extravagant funster.

I recalled this tiny incident along with many others as I contributed to the BBC's reflections on Donald's tragic death. It is remarkable how stunning developments of this nature generate their own atmosphere. There is a common thread of sadness, of loss, of personal and family grief - but also a distinctive, individual momentum.

When John Smith died, that momentum featured a feeling that our leading politicians are placed under too great a strain. For a time, it seemed as if there would be a common drive to reduce that strain.

This element was present with Donald Dewar's death. Plus, of course, the shattering sense of bereavement - of a lost leader. But the distinctive touch was anecdotal. Collectively, those who knew him well and those who knew him only slightly seemed to feel the need to swap stories.

As I followed or perhaps helped form this mood - on BBC television and radio - I felt anxious. In breaks between broadcasts, I consulted colleagues, friends, politicians. Did it sound too flippant? Were smiles and even laughter inappropriate alongside the sombre mood, the serious tributes?

No, I was repeatedly assured. It matched the man exactly. Anyone who came in contact with him bore testimony to his humanity, his humour, his wide range of interests, his intellect, his charming eccentricity, his - how to phrase it - uniquely blunt approach to inter-personal skills.

To depict him as merely a skilled politician, as merely a sizeable cog in the machine, would be to miss the man.

For a broadcast journalist - hardened by ludicrous deadlines - he could be a perfect pest. The machine politician would sweep through a photocall before delivering a suitably anodyne comment to camera.

Not Donald. He once kept a pacing posse of journalists waiting for more than half an hour in a carpet factory while he pursued his fascination with the various international forms of weaving in the company of bewildered but grateful staff. It was charming and endearing - but not, I have to say, on the day itself.

Who else but D. Dewar would regularly disarm disputatious opponents with the judicious use of the Scots language? For a number of years, I helped baffled Hansard reporters in the Commons translate the better Dewarisms.

Who else but Donald would lace his speeches with quotations from Scottish literature and precedents from history - without the need for back-up researchers?

It is entirely wrong, however, to depict him as some species of effete or eccentric intellectual, above politics, above party. Donald was intensely partisan. He had made his choice within politics and was determined to see that choice thrive. But thrive fairly. Absolutely no underhand tricks.

Equally, like all politicians with senior responsibility, he was frequently troubled by doubt. This modern media age demands that political leaders gloss their public performance with a patina of certainty.

Donald fretted that the pace of delivery under devolution was inevitably lagging behind public expectations which had been artificially heightened by the need to win support for the project in the first place. He agonised over issues ranging from exams to the Holyrood building project.

In return, friends worried over his work-rate and his frequently chaotic attitude to the basic necessities of life. I recall one such discussion when two of his Parliamentary colleagues threatened to descend upon his Glasgow home with the purpose of providing home-cooked scrambled eggs, force-fed if necessary.

Donald attracted a remarkably complex range of responses. Friends, quite simply, loved the man. Constituents likewise. Colleagues were intensely loyal - both in Scotland and London - with the very occasional exception of second-rank whispering which evaporated like noxious gas when confronted with the man's integrity and stature.

Civil servants were devoted to him, far beyond the duty of service which they would owe to any Minister. They found in him an ideal combination of inspirational leadership and close attention to the critical detail of governmental life. Personally and professionally, they held him in the very highest regard.

As for me, in seeking to sum up, I'm tempted to depart from my customary affectation of whimsy in search of something more grandiose, more sonorous.

But I sense over my shoulder a looming, gaunt, smiling presence - glancing at my efforts and snorting with affectionate derision. OK, Donald, you win. You usually did - eventually. Let's just leave it at statesman, scholar, friend.

# ALF YOUNG
*The Herald (12 October)*

First there is the raw realisation that we will never see him again. Never greet that familiar stringy, gaunt, slightly stooped figure crunching his way up our drive from one of a series of small, run-of-the-mill cars - red bodywork typically - that served as his transport and mobile office down the years.

Months after an election campaign the windows would still carry the remnants of Vote Labour posters, the back seat would still be littered with surplus leaflets and well-thumbed electoral registers.

He would arrive in his regulation V-neck sweater, often threadbare at the elbow, seldom tieless but sometimes sporting an unlikely pair of plimsolls, occasionally in a black mood, seeking only companionship, food, gossip and the chance to be himself for a few happy hours.

Down the years ours was one of what Donald called his "safe houses", the homes of a circle of close friends where he could put the remorseless pressures of his high-profile political existence aside, emerge from his darker moments, join in family life, sit on the floor if he felt like it and share confidences without fear his trust would be breached.

Whole evenings would go by without party politics ever being mentioned.

There were books and pictures to be discussed; new finds to be admired or summarily dismissed - Donald could be blunt if a print or a pot offended his tastes; sporting achievements to be celebrated; stories to be swopped about what family and mutual friends were up to.

Central to these small shared pleasures was food. Much has been made of Donald's gargantuan appetite. But 'The Gannet' was a discriminating foodie.

Donald could spend fifteen minutes debating the relative merits of fennel or celeriac. He could tease those who fed him about the quality of their latest offering. More often there was ready praise and a willing acceptance of seconds. Always there was implicit acknowledgement that breaking bread together was fundamental to true friendship.

He watched the Euro 2000 final with us, a supper plate of grilled cod perched on his knee, animatedly debating tactics with one of our sons and displaying his formidable knowledge of the beautiful game.

On a previous visit, about to go off on a ministerial visit to Japan the next day, Donald confessed that he didn't have a serviceable suitcase to his name. Shamefacedly, he asked if we had one he could borrow.

A rummage in our loft located a small blue case my mother had passed on to us. He seized it eagerly. "At least you can turn up at our Tokyo embassy without feeling embarrassed," ventured Carol. "Oh, I don't care about that," he retorted. "I was just worried I would scatter my clothes all over the airport."

We first became close in the 1970s when I was working for the Labour Party and Donald, between Westminster seats and working in the administration of the new Children's Hearing system, was one of the principal keepers of the Home Rule flame within the party.

It is easy to forget how fractured Labour was in those days on the case for a devolved Scottish parliament. No one did more to try and deliver the 1979 referendum vote than Donald. But to no avail. And no one took more pleasure two decades on when the home rule which, in Donald's own words, had survived as a hope and a belief, was turned into a promise and then a reality.

The previous year, 1978, we had managed to get him back into parliament against formidable odds, at the Glasgow Garscadden by-election. All six council seats in the constituency were held by the nationalists.

Mid-afternoon on the day of the vote, Drumchapel was awash with SNP posters and it began to snow. Donald's confidence began to slide. "It's going," he predicted, as we emerged from an old folks home.

He was wrong. And the principal reason, I believe to this day, was Donald's own exceptional ability to strike up a bond of trust with others, from hard-pressed shoppers in Drumchapel to the great and good at an Edinburgh Castle reception.

We had been through a lot together in that by-election, including a sustained personalised campaign by anti-abortionists that, in my memory, makes the more recent Section 2A furore seem a relatively tame affair. We were about to endure more, I as his constituency chairman, during the bitter re-selection battles after Labour lost the 1979 election.

I gave up politics for journalism. But anyone who was with Donald Dewar through those tough times knew that he was never a fair-weather politician, willing to trim what he believed in to the fashions or pressures of the moment.

A lot has been made of his all-consuming passion for politics. That was not the Donald I knew. I remember us slipping away from a Perth party conference to wonder at Alasdair Steven's treasure trove of antiquarian books in the wing of a ruined mansion in Glen Lyon. Or a family visit to painter James Fullarton's studio in Straiton followed by high tea at Nardini's in Largs.

Donald was also driven by a gregarious love of the company of others and an unquenchable wonder at the achievements of the human spirit.

While Donald was fighting for his life on Tuesday evening we were oblivious to his plight, in Argyll, in Knapdale, just a few miles away from the birthplaces of two of his oldest friends, John Smith and the Herald leader writer Bob McLaughlan, both also now dead.

As we drove along a finger of Loch Sween towards Tayvallich in search of supper, the late October sun lit up the spectacular gold and russet tints on the opposite bank. A solitary swan slid effortlessly across the inky glass surface of the water.

Donald would have relished that supper of scallops and smoked fish. But he would have relished too the awesome beauty of this small nation for which, in death, some offer him celestial paternity. Those of us who had the privilege to know and share friendship with the private Donald Dewar feel only desolation today. For now the void he leaves in our lives seems incapable of being filled.

# ROBERT McNEIL
*Scotsman (12 October)*


Every Thursday afternoon, Donald Dewar used to walk with a slow, stork-like gait into the chamber of The Scottish Parliament. HIS Scottish parliament.

Members' question time was generally under way, and all eyes would turn to watch the First Minister's unhurried entrance.

He never looked fazed or ruffled, no matter the crisis.

I hope it does not sound trite to say that, to a sketch-writer, Donald's death is a grievous blow because he brought the chamber alive.

He was a sublime parliamentarian with a keen sense of the ridiculous. I recall the time he read out with relish a newspaper article by a member of the opposition. "It calls to mind the literary efforts of Michael Howard or Peter Lilley," he said.

Oh, he could be so sarcastic. Once, after mockingly describing someone's speech as "tremendously clever", he was barracked by an outraged opposition. "Aw, come on," he said, indicating that he was only having fun. It was this sense of fun that so endeared him to the press and MSPs of all parties.

For all the flak, he actually enjoyed the job. He brought to it a great literary awareness, and could calm a tumult with a telling phrase. Witness the occasion when opposition members were yet again outraged. He looked up calmly and compared the noise to "a cliff of seagulls".

It was so often the case that, when all around were losing their heads, Big Donald sat there blowing out his cheeks, while a wise or witty riposte took shape in his mind.

He did not like rude or overblown language in the chamber. Under the pressure of the hauliers' blockade, he chose words like "disappointing", "unfair" and even "unpleasant" to describe the situation.

Indeed, he had a keen sense of propriety. On one occasion, he became comically befuddled, having described a fellow MSP as "Honourable Member" - a Westminster convention. He then said he hadn't meant to call him honourable at all, before explaining that he was not saying he was dishonourable. "That was merely an attempt to recover etiquette."

He also ticked off anyone who referred to "Blair" or even "Thatcher", as he thought this unacceptably impolite.

He loved quaint, antiquarian turns of phrase, referring to newspapers as "the public prints" and inadvertently reduced the whole chamber to helpless laughter when, reading transcripts of the Lobbygate tapes, he repeatedly pronounced "yeah" as "yea".

But he had gravitas aplenty and was a tremendously authoritative figure. His self-penned speech at the parliament's opening, with its references to the land and the shipyards, to "the wild cry of the great pipes", and to the battles of Bruce and Wallace, revealed his passion for his country.

Death will have his day, as Shakespeare said. But did it have to come so soon, depriving a small country of a big man?

# IAN BELL
*Business am (12 October)*

The long journey was as personal as it was political. First, a young Donald Dewar persuaded himself; then, in time, he helped to persuade his riven party. Finally, triumphantly, he convinced his country of its right to its own, restored Parliament within the United Kingdom. No Scottish politician achieved more in the 20th century.

At the end of the march Mr Dewar did not just create an institution. He gave it a character and a style, negotiated a historic shift towards more honest voting systems, forged its coalition politics and, above all, ensured that a reconvened Scottish legislature would not, could not, ever be dissolved again.

Only a great parliamentarian - painstaking, witty, incisive, profoundly learned - could have done one tenth of that.

Donald Dewar was a politician and, conspicuously, a human being. The dishevelled suits, the ums and ahs, the jokes at his own expense and that legendary appetite for every foodstuff known to man might have been anathema to the spin doctors. For Scots of every stripe they were the fabric of an authentic personality.

Political reporters might dismiss other parliamentarians by their surnames: he was always, universally, just "Donald". They could try to honour him as the Father of the Nation; he would grimace, flap a bony hand, and leave you convinced that Scotland had in fact acquired a somewhat distracted uncle.

Donald Dewar was a complex man, probably often lonely in the long aftermath of a marriage breakdown yet guarded always by deeply loyal friends. Middle class by upbringing and education at Glasgow Academy, he was also utterly at ease with his working class constituents. A formidably learned bibliophile who preferred the company of a book to fools whom he did not suffer at all, far less gladly, he was nevertheless a ruthless political operator. As Lord Forsyth, once the Tory arch-enemy, remarked yesterday, Mr Dewar was above all a conviction politician.

He was trusted for that first and last. If Labour in Scotland survived the upheavals of Blairite modernisation more or less intact that was because its leader acted as its personal guarantor. Even amid municipal sleaze, backstabbing party tribalism and Executive error "Donald" earned the belief of Labour voters and the respect of Labour's opponents. They knew he was the real thing.

He earned the honour. Never a fiery politician - suspicious, indeed, of the very idea - he won Aberdeen South in 1966, lost it again, and had to wait impatiently to be returned at Glasgow Garscadden in 1978. In Labour's wilderness years, after the great shock of the 1979 referendum, he kept faith with devolution and proved his own reliability as a politician with an eye for detail. From 1983 to 1992 he led for Labour on Scottish Affairs. For three years he was social security spokesman, then Chief Whip. In 1997, finally, he was Scottish Secretary and in that year could read from his own Bill and declare: "There shall be a Scottish Parliament."

Those of us who wrote, often enough, that devolution was inevitable did him less than credit at the time. Mr Dewar saw John Smith's "unfinished business" as a matter of duty but that alone did not conjure a Scottish Parliament out of the mist. Months and years of intense hard work were involved.

Hour upon hour spent poring over mind-numbing detail were needed. The long, convoluted negotiations that went into the Scottish Constitutional Convention had to be undergone. The skills of a superb parliamentary draftsman were required to produce, first, a White Paper, then the Scotland Bill. Above all, Mr Dewar needed the vision of which politicians so often speak but rarely possess. It took vision to see that Labour's self-serving detestation of voting reform would have to be overcome.

It took vision to allow him to accept that common cause would have to be made with the Scottish Nationalist Party if a Yes-Yes vote was to be achieved in the referendum. Vision, above all, was the potent faculty needed to convince Scots that devolution was not simply a way to suppress national aspirations, as so many in his party hoped and still hope, but a true means of national self-expression.

Donald Dewar lived the paradox: he was for the Union always, but he was also a patriot who knew more about Scotland, its history and its people, than many self-professed Nationalists.

He distrusted excess in thought and expression: that was Scottish. He valued learning and education as Scots so often do. He had ideas of social solidarity and of the nation as a community which have been the mark of the Scottish middle class. He was canny and cautious, undeniably so, in a way that Scots tend to expect from their legal practitioners. He believed in the values of sheer hard work and plain dealing and he was conscious, above all, of his identity as a Scot.

He hated fuss, even at the end, and he would not have thanked you for all the credit he deserved for home rule. In his book it was the voters who did him credit: everything else was superfluous. The black irony of dying too soon, much as his old friend John Smith had died, would not have been lost on a man who savoured irony, but the knowledge of what he and his former leader achieved for Scotland was probably its own reward. His parliament meant everything.

Mr Dewar can be faulted for failing to settle the question of a successor after his heart operation. He can be accused, with justice, of failing to delegate and failing to see the dangers of overwork. He can be faulted for excessive caution, for refusing to understand the huge expectations placed upon home rule. None of that matters now. Scotland was led to its parliament by an archetypal Scot and only now, perhaps, does it understand what it has lost.

At 12.18 yesterday rain was lashing Edinburgh. The gloom was palpable. But consider: "There shall be a Scottish Parliament." There is and shall be for generations still to come. Donald Campbell Dewar made it so.

# TOM BROWN
*Daily Record (October 12)*

Donald Dewar's place in the history books is assured. And unlike many politicians, it will not be a footnote but a full chapter of real achievement.

That would have pleased him since he was a man who cared about history. He was never more content than when he was sitting in his cluttered study, immersed in an antiquarian book - especially if it was a book on Scottish history.

Unfortunately, Donald died before anyone got round to writing his biography. If ever a man deserved to have his life story told it was him.

From his earliest years until his final struggle, that life led in one direction - into politics and the job that changed Scotland, giving his country a new direction.

He was sometimes called "Donald Dour" and "Donald Dull". Certainly it took a lot to get him to unbutton and speak about his lonely childhood and, often, lonelier adulthood.

It was in a remarkably frank interview with Daily Record reporter Simon Houston during 1998 that he spoke of his childhood of "turmoil" and "loneliness".

When he was a small boy, his surgeon father and his mother were both in poor health. His father developed TB and his mother was recovering from brain surgery, so Donald was shuttled between boarding schools across Scotland.

At fee-paying Glasgow Academy, he said he stuck out like a sore thumb because of his glasses and the accent he had acquired from mainly English schoolmates. "It was a very difficult adjustment" he recalled. "I was a quiet boy with spectacles and not much confidence."

As an only child, he felt at a loss without brothers or sisters around to back him up. His closest friend was a black-and-white Dutch rabbit which he kept at stables near his home in the West End.

During the 1955 General Election, he went to school with a Labour poster under his blazer. He said of the moment: "The authorities regarded me more as an amiable misfit than a threat."

But he was not complaining. He recalled: "I can think of kids who, just because of their expectation of failure, because of unemployment and poverty, have never had the chance that I had."

But it was when he went to Glasgow University that Donald blossomed. He said of his time there: "That was when the politics started seriously and genuinely. I found myself in the middle of a very lively group of colleagues and made friends for life."

Those friends, as one historic class picture showed, included the late John Smith, who later became Labour leader; Liberal Democrat Menzies Campbell, then sporting his Olympic athlete's blazer; and future radio tycoon Jimmy Gordon, who is now a lord. Others at the university at the same time included broadcasters Colin Mackay and Donald McCormick and - fatefully for Donald - Derry Irvine, who is now Lord Chancellor.

Donald also met fellow-student Alison McNair, who he married in 1964. She went on to help him campaign for election in Aberdeen South in 1966.

The gangly, side-burned young lawyer won the seat from the Tory Lady Tweedsmuir and for the next four years showed the concern for his constituency that became his trademark.

Four years later, he lost Aberdeen South and it seemed his life fell apart politically and personally. Alison, who was by then the mother of his two beloved children Alison and Ian, left him for their friend and politician Derry Irvine.

In a rare comment on his years of enforced bachelorhood, Donald said: "I am not against the institution of matrimony and I don't regard life as a desert. I have lots of good friends and anything can happen. I am lucky in that I get to meet lots of people."

And it was only a matter of time before Scottish Labour's rising star returned to the Commons. In 1978 he won the Garscadden by-election, holding it in the middle of the Labour government's defeat at the general election the following year. Having devoted much of his political life to the cause of devolution, he was in the forefront of the "Yes" campaign in the 1979 referendum.

It was a bitter disappointment when the devo dream was thwarted by the introduction of an artificial threshold and, with John Smith, he vowed to fight on until Scotland achieved self-government.

After the shattering blow of Smith's death, he surprised everyone by becoming a brilliant Chief Whip for Tony Blair.

His reward after the 1997 general election triumph was the job he longed for, Scottish Secretary and the chance to pilot the Scotland Act through Westminster and create The Scottish Parliament.

Donald picked up the baton laid down by John Smith - what he always spoke of as the "unfinished business" of devolution and "the settled will of the Scottish people".

When the time came for the formal choice of a Scottish Labour leader and First Minister, the party gave Donald 99.8 per cent backing - a figure which showed any other choice was inconceivable.

But there were times when his dream job turned into a nightmare. Just before last year's Scottish election, his personal ratings dropped amid charges that his team were not coping with an SNP onslaught. But his popularity was quickly restored.

The opening of the Parliament was another triumph, made memorable by two Donald Dewar moments.

First, he read the opening words of the Scotland Act with relish: "There SHALL be a Scottish Parliament", adding: "I like that."

Second, he ambled alongside the Queen with his hands in his pockets. Naturally, no offence was taken because it was just too typically Donald. Achieving a Scottish Government was one thing, but running it was another.

A string of internal crises, resignations of aides in embarrassing circumstances, policy fumbles and accusations of misjudgment led to accusations that he had become "Donald Dither". He was forced to issue denials that he was thinking of stepping aside, saying: "It's a very different job, but it's a more satisfying one."

It would be nice if the history books also had space to record the private side of Donald Dewar - a man who was surrounded by his many friends and the son and daughter who stayed so close to him.

The Donald Dewar who never wore a coat and had to famously pinch one from a colleague to visit the Lockerbie disaster. He was even once forced to buy one for the Scottish Election, but left it on a bus somewhere.

And the Donald Dewar who hated sound-bites and political stunts, but was happy to call the numbers at bingo sessions in his constituency.

As his friend Menzies Campbell said: "He stood head and shoulders above other people - and that wasn't just because he was a tall man."

# CHARLIE ALLAN
*The Herald (October 12)*

For about four years between the ages of perhaps eight and twelve, Donald came to our farm in Aberdeenshire for holidays which I remember as being long and fun. Dr Dewar, who seemed old, showed us how to make better bows and arrows and even made a split cane fishing rod out of bamboo. He designed treasure hunts for us. And Mary, who was beautiful, brought sweeties.

But mostly we two were left to our own play with the half dozen or so cottar bairns who by chance were all boys. We swam in the North Sea, caught bandies with nets in the river Ythan and made traps for trout out of the empty wine bottles which our parents generated in abundance during those visits. We chased the pigeons in the barn till they dropped and we could wring their necks.

We played kick-the-cannie, tak-ye, and heist-the-green-flag. We fought with insults and stones.

There were hours and hours of football for which Donald had some inclination but no aptitude.

It wasn't an easy environment for the boy from Glasgow who had been at a boarding school (Beverley School near Bonchester Bridge) from about five years old because both his parents were too ill to look after him. His mother had a brain tumour and I was told that his father had had TB. He couldn't speak the Doric and "talking" was a distinct disadvantage in Buchan in those days.

And yet, when the year came that it was announced that a family holiday would be enjoyed somewhere else Donald cried so much that the plans were changed and he came again to the farm.

Donald was different from the rest of us. He could read, for a start, and I don't just mean a few words. At eight years old he could read whole books without pictures. He seemed to know all of Scotland's history as well as much of its literature. When he was back in Glasgow we loons played at "Bobbies and Burglars". But when Donald came for his holidays we had William Wallace, Edward Long Shanks, the Duke of Montrose, John Knox, Alan Breck and, best of all, Colin Campbell, the Red Fox.

Instead of the typical bairns' housie Donald designed a grand fort. It had a drawbridge, represented by a bentwood frame which we could raise or lower with a rope. But this was such a pest to operate that Donald decided we should just creep in round the back and save the drawbridge for the arrival of "distinguished visitors" only. I think about that often and the irony that he was the only one of us then who knew what 'distinguished' meant and the only one who came remotely close to becoming himself "distinguished".

He was so well read that I asked Donald Dewar when he was studying Law at Glasgow University why he had not done History. With all his knowledge I thought it would have been a cushy number for him as well as being in line with his interests. He told me that he had intended to read history but that he had been put right off by the first lecture. In that the professor had said that to understand European History you had to know about an important family. He then wrote the word HABSBURG in block capitals on the board and told them to note the spelling. Donald couldn't see how this course was going to teach him much. I'm sure he was right.

The young Dewar was not what is now called 'touchy feelie'. Duty kisses for old aunties were out. He was not above letting his intellectual superiority show and he could be bated into a rage. The charm and the patience with fools, which I found so unusual and so appealing in his political personae, came later.

His mother always brought sweeties. Because I ate so quickly she divided them in half. And so developed a keen competition to see who could make them last longest. I might have beaten the budding First Minister at football but when it came to still having lots of sweeties left long after I had finished mine, he was the master.

The other part of my boyhood relationship with Donald Dewar is more vivid for me because then I was the stranger. I stayed with him in Glasgow on at least three occasions.

By this time he had left boarding school and was attending Glasgow Academy. There he had been introduced to the mysteries of rugby football. Donald seemed to find it easier to play with an oval ball than a round one. He showed his country cousin how to tackle properly with a most convincing demonstration. He grabbed me round the waist and told me to run away. This I did rather effectively. But when he grabbed me by the ankles I couldn't move one inch. I see him clearly still, on the floor in the corridor of his parents' flat in Lacrosse Terrace, my ankles trapped and he looking earnestly up at me to be sure that I had got the point of 'tackling low'.

Donald took me to see Glasgow Academicals tackling low at Anniesland, and to see George Young, Tiger Shaw and Willie Waddell at Ibrox. But he was curiously embarrassed by his affection for the Glasgow Rangers and told me several times that he was a Partick Thistle supporter really, as Firhill was just up the road.

But what I remember best was the bizarre fight that Donald organised for me. He had this acquaintance who came from Partick on the other side of the river Kelvin. He was not only tough but the leader of a small gang. Donald encouraged me that I too was quite tough and might manage to handle him.

The venue was the back green of the tenement. I was introduced to Tom and we proceeded to fight. I can vouch for the fact that he was strong but thank goodness he wasn't nasty. In fact, as fighters go, he was very nice to me.

Under the watchful eye of the future First Minister he would wrestle me to the ground, establish mastery and then let me get up saying, "fair's fair", whereupon he would knock me down again.

In the fifty years in which I knew Donald subsequently the great fight was never mentioned so I am only guessing. But I think that while Donald was quite proud of the plucky show his friend from the country had put up, he was even more proud of the way that Tom had shown me how tough Glasgow was.

I often produce tears. It only takes a sentimental passage in a book, the sight of Steve Redgrave winning his fifth gold medal, or my old friend walking with the Queen at the opening of his life's work, and down they roll. But I can only remember twice in my life crying. The second time was when I heard the official announcement on Radio Scotland that Donald was dead. And I don't really think I was crying for those boyhood days. I think I was crying for Scotland. Our devolved status could so easily descend into chaos and we don't have a queue of Donald Dewars waiting to take his place.